MASTERS OF SOCIAL PSYCHOLOGY

MASTERS OF
SOCIAL PSYCHOLOGY
FREUD, MEAD, LEWIN, AND SKINNER

James A. Schellenberg

New York

OXFORD UNIVERSITY PRESS

1978

301.1092
S 322 m
c - 1
9.95
7178

Library of Congress Cataloging in Publication Data

Schellenberg, James A   1932-
Masters of social psychology

Bibliography: p.
Includes index.
1. Social psychology—Addresses, essays, lectures.
2. Psychologists—Biography. I. Title.
HM251.S2993   301.1′092′2   77-9927
ISBN 0-19-502278-5
ISBN 0-19-502279-3 pbk.

To Chris

Contents

Preface

This little book has been many years aborning. From the time I first read Robert Heilbroner's *The Worldly Philosophers* I have thought off and on of doing something for behavioral science similar to what he did for economics. Heilbroner presented the theories of economics through an examination of the lives of the great economists. This struck me as an effective way of giving some flesh and bones to otherwise rather abstract subject matter. But then I became involved in writing and revising a social psychology textbook, and this, plus my more routine teaching and research activities, crowded out plans for another book.

Then came my 1974–75 sabbatical leave from Western Michigan University. I was interested in spending the year in Ireland, and had arranged to take on some teaching duties in social psychology at the New University of Ulster, Coleraine, Northern Ireland, and at University College, Cork. But what was I to teach? The social psychology I had put in my textbook seemed to me too thoroughly American to present in another land. Besides, I approached my Irish assignment with a somewhat exaggerated impression of the awesome role of the lecturer and the intellectual level of students in universities on the European side of the Atlantic. So, during the summer of 1974 I carefully prepared a different approach, introducing social psychology through the lives and thoughts of some leading theorists. I included Marx and Piaget (as well as the four masters in the present book) to demonstrate my acquaintance with European theorists and to show the continuity between social psychology and neighboring disciplines. What I wanted to avoid at all costs was to come in as the "ugly American" who only had an ethnocentric social psychology to share.

As it turned out, I was wrong. Irish students were not that different from those in America. And far from resenting something from America, the Irish I met—both in the north and in the south—seemed to me more pro-American than were my friends in the United States. Nevertheless, I had my lectures prepared, so I used them. Returning to Western Michigan University in the fall of 1975, I found these lectures useful in an advanced social psychology class. At that time I began planning their revision into the form they now take.

In acknowledging, therefore, those who made this book possible, I want to mention first of all the students—at Coleraine, Cork, and Kalamazoo—who suffered through the lectures that represented the original draft. Their questions and reactions have helped to shape the work into its present form. I also want to make clear my debt to my former institution, Western Michigan University, for providing the setting in which this project could take shape.

J.A.S.

Terre Haute, Indiana
April, 1977

MASTERS OF SOCIAL PSYCHOLOGY

I

PARADIGMS AND PARABLES

"Practical men," the economist John Maynard Keynes once observed, "who believe themselves to be quite exempt from any intellectual influences, are usually the slaves of some defunct economist." In the same vein, he wrote, "madmen in authority, who hear voices in the air, are distilling their frenzy from some academic scribbler of a few years back" (quoted by Heilbroner, 1961, p. 2).

As with economics and politics, so too is it with ideas of social psychology. A person for whom Freud is only a faintly familiar word may talk glibly about repressed wishes or the need to find an outlet for aggression, thus reflecting central assumptions about Sigmund Freud's theories. Others who have never heard of G. H. Mead or Kurt Lewin will nevertheless state truisms about social behavior, picked up somewhere from reading or listening, that embody key ideas of these social psychologists. And to explain social behavior on the basis of past reinforcement—even using this central term of modern be-

haviorism—has become commonplace for millions who only
vaguely associate the name of B. F. Skinner with the science
of psychology.

What some of the great social psychologists have said has
entered into our everyday discussion of social behavior. It is
not only that we use some of their terms, but we have also absorbed something of the perspectives within which these terms
have become meaningful. But herein lies a problem. We have
absorbed these perspectives in a rather jumbled manner. There
is confusion about how these different theories fit together.

The confusion of our everyday theories of social behavior
also has its counterpart in the discipline of social psychology.
One of the difficulties in introducing people to social psychology
is that there is not a single general perspective within which
all its theories fit. There are a number of different perspectives,
none of which is at present dominant. Or to use a term which
has lately (especially since Kuhn [1962]) gained currency,
social psychology is a science without a single unifying "paradigm." It has several fundamentally different ways of conceiving its subject matter and pursuing its research. That social
psychology is a multi-paradigm science may be glossed over by
its introductory textbooks, but this fact remains a source of
strain and confusion to those learning to work in the field.

There are several fundamentally different ways to "do science" in social psychology, reflecting different leading theoretical perspectives. Among these perspectives are at least the following four:

• The psychoanalytic approach, which seeks for causes of
social behavior in inner emotional forces of the individual;
• the symbolic interactionist perspective, which sees behavior
as subjectively determined within a specifically social context;

• the gestalt approach, which emphasizes present cognitive organization as a basis of behavior;
• the behaviorist perspective, which considers present behavior as a product of particular features of past behavior.

Each of these approaches has developed its own typical research procedures. Also, each is especially associated with key contributions of a few individuals. In fact, in terms of overall influence upon contemporary social psychology, it is fairly easy to select one individual who is most predominantly identified with each of the above approaches. These individuals are the masters of social psychology who provide the primary subject matter for this book.

As a young doctor in Vienna carefully probed his patients' psyches for emotional associations with their forms of illness, he gradually came to build a theory about unconscious psychological forces. Thus came into being the practice and theory (in that order of appearance) of psychoanalysis. Later this same doctor, Sigmund Freud, became especially interested in processes of social influence, and so psychoanalysis became applied to basic questions of social psychology. The result was not only a rich variety of clinical insights, but also the most intellectually exciting theory of socialization known to modern social science.

At about the same time an American professor explored with his philosophy students what is distinctive about human nature. This professor came to conceive that the interaction between individuals, enhanced by the development of symbolic expression, provided the primary building material for human selves. His theories about this process made George H. Mead the central figure in that stream of social psychology generally known as symbolic interactionism. This perspective,

especially popular among social psychologists with a sociological background, has been widely applied in studies of socialization, small group behavior, and the impact of institutional settings.

As a Jewish refugee from Nazi Germany came to America,
he brought with him a highly contagious enthusiasm for theory
building and a passion for social reform. In America these
talents of Kurt Lewin became directed toward a new synthesis.
This synthesis, known as "field theory," was inspired by
Lewin's German roots in gestalt psychology, but it also had a
distinctively American flavor as it developed into group dynamics and action research. Contemporary social psychology
in the United States has been more powerfully influenced by
Lewin and his students than by any other comparable group.

B. F. Skinner has pursued a very different style of work
from that of Freud, Mead, or Lewin. His technological bent
and philosophy of radical behaviorism led Skinner to a much
simpler model for looking at social behavior. Nevertheless, the
operant behaviorism Skinner first developed in his studies of
rats caged in the laboratories of Harvard has worked a major
revolution in twentieth-century psychology. A leading factor
in this revolution has been Skinner's own concern with applying his model to complex forms of human behavior. The full
impact of these efforts is just now beginning to be felt in social
psychology.

Of course there are many other men and women who have
made major contributions to psychoanalysis, symbolic interactionism, field theory, and operant behaviorism. As pioneers,
however, Freud, Mead, Lewin, and Skinner stand out. Our
attention will therefore focus on these four men. Each clearly
represents a different framework, a different paradigm, for en-
gaging in the science of social psychology.

At the outset of this chapter we quoted Lord Keynes on the powerful impact of economists and political philosophers upon popular thought. We implied that the same point would apply to the influence of leading social psychologists, at least for those we have prepared to designate as "masters." We now want to underline this point further, with special reference to the continuity between what the social psychologist studies and what are concerns in everyday life.

As the new science of social psychology has emerged in the twentieth century—where the older disciplines of sociology and psychology overlap in the study of interpersonal behavior—it has developed its own specialized theories and research procedures. A sampling of its basic literature in such places as the *Journal of Personality and Social Psychology,* the *Journal of Experimental Social Psychology,* or *Sociometry* could prove to the layman that it can be almost as unintelligible as the next science. Almost, but not quite, for there is always in social psychology a concern for basic questions shared by most men and women. These questions may be phrased differently from the language of laymen, and the research may lead to different observations from those of everyday life. But at the back of the social psychologist's work are such fundamental questions as the following: How do we learn to become functioning members of society? How are we influenced by others in ongoing interaction? How is our thought and behavior affected by particular features of society, such as those reaching us through the mass media or through the activities of certain groups?

These questions are also of direct concern to most men and women as they go about their lives; and this makes for a common bond between the science of social psychology and a great deal of informal observation of ordinary people. Social psychologists often feel uncomfortable about this link to the layman. They take some pains to point out how their hypotheses and findings depart from common sense. Certainly their more specialized efforts distinguish features and observe nuances of behavior never imagined by most people. But behind these differences between the science of social psychology and the popular psychology of everyman is usually a common theme. Both search for broad truths about social behavior, truths that can be appreciated by scientist and citizen alike.

Milton J. Rosenberg has made a similar point by referring to the "parable" function of many experiments in social psychology. Just as general social-science theories may serve for many as secular theologies—ways we can conceive of our place and purpose within a social universe—so in a similar manner the particular experiments social psychologists perform may be seen as parables. To use Rosenberg's words, they "give voice, in concretized representation, to some large, life-organizing truths—and do so in a dramatized form that stirs the 'shock of recognition,' the shudder of insight" (Rosenberg, 1970, p. 181). They are, in other words, concrete expressions on a small scale of some larger truth about human experience; and what the experiment demonstrates is not only what the investigator explicitly points out, but also this larger truth which is usually implicit in the discussion of the experiment.

As Rosenberg indicates, some of the best-known examples of research in social psychology (Solomon Asch's studies of conformity, Stanley Milgram's work on obedience, and Leon Festinger's cognitive dissonance experiments, for examples) may be viewed in this light. All of these present in sharply illuminated form some basic idea about our nature as social animals, such as that we are overly prone to conform to our peers, to accept the dictates of authority, and frequently to become irrational in the way we justify our actions.

What holds true for particular experiments also applies to

more general theories. In their experiments social psychologists often take a piece of our common experience to illuminate a more general idea. In their theories they take some common conception about human social life and express it in more formal and logically precise terms. In substance, though, there is a basic continuity between what social psychologists think about and what may occupy the thoughts of ordinary citizens.

To point to the continuity between the ideas of social psychologists and laymen is not, however, to say that social psychologists simply borrow their theories from the common assumptions of everyday life. To be sure, some—such as Fritz Heider (1958)—have argued that the social psychologist can learn much from studying the naive psychology with which people commonly form their actions. But for the most part emphasis has come from the other direction; the theories come from the past writings of scholars who have given more systematic formulations of ideas than could be popularly conceived. Social psychologists borrow from these scholars, adding those emphases that fit the research each knows best.

In this introductory chapter we have so far made two main points. First, there are several different frameworks, or paradigms, prominent in social psychology, and each is especially associated with an influential theorist. Second, the issues of leading theories in social psychology show a close continuity with key questions we ask in everyday life. Both of these feed into a third major point. The full meaning of a major approach in social psychology is best grasped if we examine the living context in which it was formed. Therefore, rather than starting with the discussion of a leading theory, then adding some information incidentally about the theorist, we will proceed in the opposite direction. We will first present biographical data to show the living context in which a theory was formed. Then we will present the main outlines of the theoretical approach as it emerged from that context. Finally, we will discuss further ramifications of each approach, especially emphasizing its impact upon contemporary social psychology.

In other words, we will start first with the lives of our masters. Keeping alert to the events associated with the development of their ideas, we should better appreciate the significance of these theories. In particular, this should sensitize us to see more clearly the relationship between the leading theories of social psychology and the events of everyday experience they may serve to enlighten.

II

SIGMUND FREUD
AND PSYCHOANALYSIS

Origins of Psychoanalysis

Sigmund Freud never set out to be a psychologist. Much less did he see himself—until quite late in life—as contributing to the field of social psychology. He was simply a Viennese physician specializing in the treatment of nervous disorders. That this activity would lead him to fundamentally new ways of conceiving social behavior was little imagined by Freud when he took up this work.

In fact, Freud was already thirty years old before he began his private practice; and his reasons for doing so were originally more financial than scientific. After an engagement of four years, Freud married Martha Bernays in the fall of 1886. He needed to provide support for his parents as well as the new family he and his new wife would be starting. It was at this time that Sigmund Freud, in search of improved financial security, embarked on his career as a private physician.

Freud had already distinguished himself as a research physiologist and neuroanatomist. He had served as junior physician at Vienna's General Hospital and had recently been appointed

as a part-time lecturer at the University of Vienna. His focus
of interest had been organic diseases of the nervous system, and
he had already made significant scientific contributions to
specifying the functions of the medulla oblongata—the base of
the brain that helps regulate vital functions such as respiration
and circulation—and studying the effects of the drug cocaine
upon the nervous system. But Freud's work at General Hospital was no more capable of supporting two families than had
been his earlier work in the physiological laboratory. So in
1886 he turned from a promising scientific career to the finan-
cially more rewarding prospects of a private practice.

Freud's initial contributions as a private physician were
hardly such as to gain him much esteem—at least so far as the
local practitioners of Vienna were concerned. To help launch
his career in the private treatment of nervous diseases he had
spent the previous winter in Paris studying under Jean Martin
Charcot. At that time Charcot was widely known for his pioneering work in the treatment of nervous diseases. He was then
especially concerned with hysteria, emphasizing psychological
causes rather than physiological conditions for this strange
medley of emotional upset and physical symptoms. Furthermore, Charcot used hypnosis in its treatment. Freud brought
back the main elements of Charcot's treatment to Vienna,
where hysteria was still considered primarily as a physiological
disturbance.

Freud saw in the treatment of hysteria a chance to make his
mark upon Viennese medical practice. However, when he reported on Charcot's work, he found the local leaders of medi-
cine either unbelieving or unimpressed. Undaunted, Freud proceeded to identify a case of hysteria in a male (where it had
only been diagnosed in females until then) and to produce
hysterical symptoms by suggestion. Both of these acts contra-
dicted the prevailing views at Vienna on hysteria, but little note

was taken of these achievements. Indeed, the reception was often hostile in the very circles where Freud had previously been most recognized. Freud then generally withdrew from contact with official medical circles of Vienna, focusing almost exclusively upon his own private practice.

One local physician who did not reject Freud's new ideas was Josef Breuer. Indeed, Breuer had himself been using hypnosis for years in the treatment of hysteria. One especially interesting case had been mentioned by Breuer to Freud before the latter had gone to study with Charcot. When he returned from Paris, Freud asked Breuer for more details on this case, which had been treated several years earlier. It involved a young woman who had become ill while nursing her dying father. The illness involved forms of paralysis and mental confusion. By chance Breuer had discovered that her confusion might be reduced after she verbalized her emotional feelings. Also he found that under hypnosis she made clear associations between her symptoms and the conditions earlier experienced with her father. Furthermore, when hypnosis had involved free expression of emotions associated with a symptom, the symptom frequently disappeared.

Later, looking back over his career, Freud traced the origins of psychoanalysis to this case and to the methods of treatment Breuer had developed in dealing with it. Although Breuer had used hypnosis, the key to his success appeared to be the way he had his patient "talk out" what was troubling her. This "cathartic" method was taken over by Freud. He would induce hypnosis and then ask his patients to talk about experiences that might be associated psychologically with the particular symptoms of illness. Freud found success with this approach, though gradually he began to have reservations concerning the use of hypnosis in this manner.

For a time Freud and Breuer worked as close colleagues.

They shared with each other their findings obtained through the use of the cathartic method, and together they wrote about their approach. Their book, *Studies on Hysteria,* was published in 1895. But by the time this work appeared, their relationship had cooled. Breuer had a very busy general practice, and there were some technical differences in the way they interpreted hysteria—Breuer gave a more physiological interpretation than did Freud, for example. However, Freud considered a much more basic factor in the split to be their different reactions to matters of sex.

About 1892 Freud abandoned the use of hypnosis for a new approach he first called the "concentration technique." He had for some time been concerned about the dependence on the physician hypnosis had created, and he was searching for a more natural and direct way to achieve the results of catharsis. With the concentration technique he would press the patient, without hypnosis, to recall experiences associated with symptoms. Gradually this developed into the technique of "free association" where the patient would simply relax and report whatever ideas would come up spontaneously. Anything mentioned by the patient might then be regarded as a possible clue to the basis of his or her disturbance. As Freud used free association he became more and more convinced of the central importance of sexual factors in neuroses. For example, he soon saw sexual conflicts as the key to understanding most hysterical symptoms, a conclusion that Breuer could not share.

Nor was Breuer prepared to deal with the intensity of feelings that came to be expressed toward the physician by patients under treatment. He, as did Freud, recognized this as a form of return to an earlier pattern of relationships, but he could not easily handle its present results. This phenomenon of "transference" (attaching to the physician the emotional value of matters uncovered in probing into the past) was becoming a central aspect of Freud's treatment. In looking back later upon Breuer's original case, Freud believed he understood the key reason for the differences with his one-time close colleague: Breuer had been unable to handle the sexual content of the transference involved in this case. Instead, revolted by what he dimly glimpsed, he brought the treatment to an abrupt conclusion.

It is ironic that in later describing how he first conceived of the sexual origin of neurosis, Freud reported receiving key inspiration from an incident with Breuer many years earlier. He and Breuer were walking along the street when a man came up and insisted on speaking with Breuer. After the man had left, Breuer explained to Freud briefly about the man's wife, whom he was treating as a nervous case. He concluded with the comment that such cases were always problems of the marriage bed. This chance comment Breuer himself forgot, but it made a deep impression upon his younger companion (Freud, 1914; rpt. 1957, pp. 11–12).

Psychoanalysis as a method of therapy may be said to have originated in the cathartic method of Breuer that Freud developed into the technique of free association. Freud first used the term "psycho-analysis" for his approach in 1896, after completely discarding the use of hypnotism. Another key technique developed early by Freud was that of dream analysis. Free association and dream anaylsis were the two basic contributions of Freud to methods of psychotherapy.

Probing the Depths

In the fall of 1896 Freud's father died at the age of eighty-one. Sigmund Freud was then forty, was well established in his medical practice, and had a family of his own. By then all six of their children had been born to Sigmund and Martha Freud, and Freud was happy and devoted in his roles as husband and father. Nevertheless, he found himself severely shaken by his father's death. As he then wrote to a friend in Berlin, "I feel now as if I had been torn up by the roots" (quoted by Costigan, 1965, p. 47).

Freud was astonished at the extent to which he was affected by this death. To help him understand his own reactions he began, the following summer, to do a psychoanalysis of himself. For subject matter he turned especially to his dreams. He had sometimes found that dreams of his patients provided keys to unconscious meanings. Now in his own dreams he confirmed this conviction of their importance. They became, as he later put it, the royal road to the unconscious.

The two years that followed were probably the most intensely productive years of Freud's life. The most direct and concrete result was the publication of *The Interpretation of Dreams* in 1900 in which Freud used his own dreams as a chief part of the subject matter. Throughout his life he always considered this book his best.

In unraveling the meaning of dreams, Freud insisted that we must distinguish between the manifest content of a dream (what it appears to be about) and its latent content (what it is really about). On the surface a dream usually seems quite silly. When we probe below the surface, however, we may begin to see an inner logic in the elements. Most of the parts of a dream are simply the residues of daily life, common features of the dreamer's everyday experience. But when we examine the inner contents, there is always one central theme which seems foreign to daily life. This represents the impulse that brings the dream into being. It is most often a forbidden impulse, one which would not be recognized consciously. Even in a dream it must be hidden behind more acceptable content. But it is nevertheless there—the repressed wish for which the dream as a whole provides fulfillment.

To see more concretely how this form of interpretation may be applied to a dream, let us take one small example from *The Interpretation of Dreams*. In the spring of 1897 Freud had a simple dream consisting of an idea and an accompanying image. As he summarized this dream (Freud, 1900; rpt. 1953, p. 137):

I. . . . My friend R. was my uncle—I had a great feeling of affection for him.
II. I saw before me his face, somewhat changed. It was as though it had been drawn out lengthways. A yellow beard that surrounded it stood out especially clearly.

At that time Freud had just heard that his name had been suggested for appointment as a part-time professor at the university. Such an appointment (which he did in fact receive five years later) would clearly be an honor, and it would entitle him to give lectures on a regular basis. The evening before his dream Freud had a visit from his friend R, whose name had for sometime been under consideration for a similar position. This friend was Jewish, as was Freud. That evening R reported on an inquiry which seemed to indicate that R's own appointment was being held up for reasons of anti-Semitic feeling.

At first Freud could see no relationship of these facts to his dream. The dream seemed to be pure nonsense. But remembering how his patients also considered many of their most revealing dreams as nonsense, he pushed on. "R was my uncle"— what could this mean? Which uncle? Immediately Freud thought of his Uncle Josef, who many years earlier had been convicted of a crime. Freud's father had described him as not a bad man but only a simpleton. And there in the dream were features of his uncle (the elongated face with beard) that had become associated with R.

Freud then saw the association between his criminal uncle and another colleague N, who had also been recommended for a professorship. N had reported that his own case might have been delayed by some earlier record of (unfounded and quickly dropped) criminal charges. The meaning then became clear. As Freud interpreted the dream, his Uncle Josef represented two colleagues who had not been appointed to professorships. One was too simple-minded, and the other had a criminal record. By denying, in his dream, that anti-Semitism was a factor in these cases, Freud could feel more confident about his own chances.

But there was still one feature of the dream unexplained. Why the "great feeling of affection" for R? It did not naturally fit Freud's relation to either his Uncle Josef or his friend R. Nor did it fit with the basic latent content of the dream. The only way Freud could solve the puzzle of this aspect was to conclude that its purpose was to conceal the true interpretation of the dream. His dream had contained a slander against his good friend, and to keep himself from noticing this the feeling of affection was created as a part of the dream (pp. 137–41).

Such probing behind the defenses of the conscious mind was typical of Freud's interpretation of dreams and, indeed, of his whole approach in psychoanalysis. Most who heard of his work were very skeptical about this approach. Freud's answer was two-sided. On the one hand, he simply went about his work of treating patients, gradually building up a clientele convinced of his curative powers. But there was also a more public side in Freud's response to skepticism about psychoanalysis: he wrote about his ideas. With the pen he hoped to share some of his pioneering efforts with a resisting world.

Shortly after the turn of the century, *The Interpretation of Dreams* was followed by a popular summary *On Dreams* (1901) and three more books in which Freud probed the depths of unconscious motives. *The Psychopathology of Everyday Life* was published in 1904 (though most of it had appeared in other forms in 1901). This work dealt with symptomatic actions such as slips of the tongue or pen which, like dreams, can be examined to reveal underlying unconscious motives. Although probably the most widely read of all of Freud's books, he himself considered this work to be distastefully formless. In 1905 two other books appeared, *Wit and Its Relation to the Unconscious* and *Three Essays on the Theory of Sexuality*. The first was a study of humor and the powerful unconscious forces that direct the expression and pleasurable feelings of jokes. The latter work contained the first systematic statement of Freud's views on infantile sexuality. Next to *The Interpretation of Dreams,* Freud considered *Three Essays on the Theory of Sexuality* as his most important work.

By 1905 Freud had established both the main techniques of psychoanalytic treatment and the main ideas of psychoanalytic theory. At the time neither the methods nor the theories of psychoanalysis were widely noted. Freud continued his writing and medical practice in relative isolation from the psychologists and physicians of his day. In Vienna in particular his ideas and methods were generally ignored, though sometimes greeted by scorn and sarcasm. A small handful of local physicians, however, were impressed by Freud's work, and they sought to apply his techniques in their own practice. They began to meet weekly at Freud's offices, and thus was born the beginnings of the psychoanalytic movement. By 1908 there were about twenty members in this group, and several from outside Vienna—Sandor Ferenczi from Budapest, Carl Jung from

Zurich, Karl Abraham from Berlin, Ernest Jones from London, and A. A. Brill from New York—had initiated contacts that were to spread psychoanalysis to leading cities around the world.

Freud's Psychic Determinism

In the process of describing how Sigmund Freud first developed the methods of treatment and their interpretation—which together came to be known as psychoanalysis—we have suggested some of the key ideas of his psychology. The importance of unconscious motives, processes of resistance and repression, the general importance of sexual factors in psychological conflicts, and the particular importance of infantile sexuality—these have been among the central ideas of Freud's psychological interpretations as formulated by the end of the first decade of the present century. We now turn to examine these ideas a little more fully in order to understand them as a basis for Freud's social psychology.

Central to all of Freud's psychological interpretations was the importance of unconscious motivation. According to Freud, "Psychoanalysis regarded everything mental as being in the first instance unconscious; the further quality of 'consciousness' might also be present, or again it might be absent" (Freud, 1925; rpt. 1959, p. 31). Thus it was the unconscious mind, not consciousness, that for him was the basis for psychology. Freud came to this conclusion early through his work with hypnosis, and, as he later expressed it, his observations "of the frequency and power of impulses of which one knew nothing directly" (pp. 31–32). The driving forces of an individual's life had to be seen as originating in some inner system of which he or she might at the most be only vaguely aware.

The basic reservoir of mental life is thus unconscious. Part of this might be accessible to consciousness without emotional resistance, and this part Freud called the "preconscious" (or "foreconscious"). Most of the unconscious, however, cannot be called into consciousness. Any move in this direction meets with resistance or censorship, with the censorship usually located by Freud in the preconscious. The unconscious is an extremely active part of the person, fundamentally consisting of strivings and impulses to action which supply the motive power for psychological experience. In contrast to the vast unconscious, the conscious part of experience was for Freud a relatively small part of the functioning person.

Early in his work Freud had noted the strong resistance patients showed to probing certain areas of their past experience. Analysis of this resistance led him to formulate a theory about "repression" (the purposive delegation of experiences to the unconscious) and what became technically known as "resistance" (keeping such experiences unconscious).

In our normal mental life there is most often some conflict between immediate impulses and other considerations. Through this conflict the energy from our impulses tends to be somewhat redirected. In some cases, however, we cannot bear to let this conflict take its course. The impulse is so threatening that it must be forced aside the moment we begin to become aware of its existence. This is what happens in the case of repression. To keep such impulses from coming into consciousness later, part of the normal energy of mental life is used to provide a constant defense against the acceptance of such impulses; and this is what Freud called resistance. The repressed impulse, however, is not eliminated by such a defensive reaction. Instead it expresses itself in indirect ways, leading to behavior that the individual is sometimes unable to explain. Neurosis occurs when such behavior is especially prominent in the life of an individual.

The material that Freud's patients seemed compelled to repress consisted largely of sexual memories and ideas. At first Freud thought he had identified traumatic sexual experiences in the early childhood of many of his patients. By about 1900, however, he had discovered that usually these events had not actually happened; they had been created instead by the imagination of his patients. In tracing the sources of this imagination, however, Freud again and again came to the importance of sexual wishes and desires—not only for adult years but for the early formative experiences of the infant as well. This led him to formulate the theory of "libido." Libido, or sexual energy, constituted one of the two great drives in the human reservoir of unconscious motives. The other, the drive for self-preservation, he called the "ego" drive. These two drives—ultimately aimed respectively at the procreation and preservation of life—Freud regarded as biologically given. The ego drive was less a problem for understanding than was the libido, for needs of self-preservation cannot be denied if one is to live. With libido, however, it is different. Sexual energy can be created without being used directly; indeed, this is typically the case with libido. The energy becomes mobilized, but it does not receive any direct release. Thus it becomes available for expression in indirect ways. These continual changes of libido thus become the main ingredients in the symptoms experienced by Freud's neurotic patients.

However, libido impels behavior for everybody, not just for neurotics, for there is no firm line separating normal and abnormal behavior. And in the process of normal development, there are characteristic patterns of development in the way libido forces express themselves. This may be seen as a series of stages of development. At the very beginning libido is not particularly organized in terms of the various functions of the body. Soon, however, it comes to relate especially to activities of the mouth, the oral stage. This is followed by an anal stage in which elimination and defecation activities become central. Finally, the genitals themselves become centers of pleasure. However, this soon leads to severe conflict, because the nearest target for sexual attention—the parent of the opposite sex—has other sources of sexual interest. There follows a systematic repression of sexual urges, producing what Freud called a period of "latency." This latency lasts until puberty brings with it a second period of genital interest, this time seeking expression outside the immediate family. Intense conflict experienced at any stage of development may lead to retardation of further development, or what Freud called a "fixation" at that stage. Even after later stages develop, problems similar to those experienced earlier may lead to a return—or, for Freud, a "regression"—to the peculiar preoccupations of that stage. Such fixations and regressions Freud found particularly common among his neurotic patients.

The Freudian concept of libido should be seen somewhat more broadly than what we commonly identify as sex. Indeed, any force primarily directed toward immediate pleasure might be considered as libido, though Freud clearly had sex in mind as its best example. The sexual instincts, broadly understood as libido, could most formally be identified as those that operated according to the "pleasure principle" of immediate gratification. This pleasure principle always functioned toward the reduction of tension in some physiological system.

In contrast to the pleasure principle of libido, Freud set forth the "reality principle," which demands adjustment to an external world. The ego instincts must learn early to adjust to the needs of an environment, and thus they come to be more easily shaped by the reality principle than is libido. For the sexual instincts the shaping of reality is less direct; they remain primarily directed to pleasure, but to pleasure which also requires some adjustment to reality. Thus, especially for sexual impulses, the stage is set for the inevitable conflict, essentially unconscious, between pleasure and reality. The forms taken by this conflict are the primary basis of the personality patterns and neurotic symptoms given central attention by psychoanalysis.

Ultimately Freud's theory of psychic energy rested on a biological base. The ego drives were directed fundamentally toward sustaining life, and the sexual drives fundamentally sought bodily pleasure. The driving force of the ego was the simple desire to stay alive, while that of libido was erotic satisfaction. But these biological forces express themselves psychologically, and, according to Freud, these psychological manifestations show a strictly determined pattern.

Freud was philosophically committed to a deterministic position. This he saw as a necessary part of the scientific attitude he affirmed. His key contribution was to indicate how unconscious psychological motives might be a crucial part of causation of human experience. Because he saw all behavior as psychologically determined—as caused by internally derived motives—we may describe Freud's views as a "psychic determinism." Even the most apparently random behavior of human beings—dreams, for example—Freud saw as determined by unconscious psychological forces in strongly patterned ways. There are thus psychic causes for all behavior, even though this may not be recognized by the conscious mind.

Freud's Social Psychology

In 1913 and 1914 Freud broke new ground which moved psychoanalysis in the direction of a social science. In addition, events over which he had little control moved him to think more and more about the social implications of his theories.

First, there was *Totem and Taboo*. On May 13, 1913, the day he completed this work, he commented in a letter to Sandor Ferenczi that he had not worked at anything with "such certainty and elation" since *The Interpretation of Dreams* (Robert, 1966, p. 299). He was well aware of the new ground he had broken by presenting a psychoanalysis of primitive morality and religion. With a bold leap of imagination he had combined anthropological data on incest avoidance and totemism in primitive tribes with the psychological dynamics of the Oedipal complex. The ambivalence of feelings primitive people express in their rites of magic and religion Freud saw as directly parallel to the ambivalence of children toward their parents, and out of both are produced taboos that control the expression of sex and aggression. Freud was even so bold as to propose that back in the mists of prehistory there may have been an actual murder of a primal patriarch by his sons, followed by the institutionalization of their remorse by taboos against murder and incest. Whether or not such events actually transpired in an early primal group, such psychic efforts to identify with parents Freud saw as the foundations of primitive—and following them, civilized—systems of morality and religion.

Freud recognized that his audacity in *Totem and Taboo* would probably help divide the psychoanalytic movement. But he was prepared for that. For some time Alfred Adler and

Carl Jung had been showing increased independence from Freud's views. The split became final in 1914 with both of these one-time disciples, and the interpretation of libido was a central issue in both cases. Adler wanted to broaden the concept of libido to apply generally to most active striving in social life, and Jung wanted to extend the concept even further to apply to almost all life energy. Jung in particular had pointed out that the libido may generally withdraw from external objects; then how could it continue to exist unless it were essentially continuous with other life forces? In defense Freud was forced to add a qualification to his libido theory. The libido may indeed withdraw from external objects and become focused on the ego. This theory of narcissism was suggested in *Totem and Taboo* and more specifically formulated the following year, but it left some theoretical problems unresolved. No longer was there a simple duality between libido drives and ego drives, but the two may become intertwined in ways that were still not fully specified.

Then, also in 1914, came the war. At its onset Freud was stirred with patriotic fervor. Austria-Hungary had, as he then said, all his libido; and he proudly saw his three sons volunteer for military duty during the opening weeks of the war. Within a few months, however, Freud's outlook had changed to one of deep pessimism, which remained his mood during most of the war. For his own immediate family and professional circle, the war brought years of privation, followed shortly after by the untimely deaths of his daughter and of a grandson who was particularly close. It was then, in 1920, that Freud announced a major revision of his theory of instincts in *Beyond the Pleasure Principle*.

In this new formulation the term "libido" became applied to the full range of energy available to support and build life. The instincts for self-preservation (ego drives) and those for preservation of the species (sexual drives) were now combined into one overall life force, "eros." Eros was all impulsive energy in support of life. It was still driven by the pleasure principle (and checked by the reality principle), but the organic base for libidinal pleasure was now conceptualized in more diffuse terms than formerly. No longer was it primarily sexual in nature. Indeed, the notion of an instinct became more broadly conceptualized as "a kind of elasticity of living things, an impulsion towards the restoration of a situation which once existed but was brought to an end by some external disturbance" (Freud, 1925; rpt. 1959, p. 57). This broader conceptualization of the nature of instincts allowed Freud to see an impulse toward death and destruction as another basic instinct. This death instinct—or "thanatos," as he named it—operated according to the "Nirvana principle," which sought a state of nothingness. The striving of the death instinct was toward the absolute zero of nothing but death. Life as we live it always includes the expression of these two fundamental instincts of life and death. As Freud expressed it, "The picture which life presents to us is the result of the concurrent and mutually opposing action of Eros and the death instinct" (p. 57).

Along with his reformulation of a theory of instincts, Freud developed a formal theory of personality, which included the tripartite division into id, ego, and superego. This was first systematically presented in *The Ego and the Id* (1923). The id is a completely unconscious reservoir of primitive energy. The ego is "that part of the id which has been modified by the direct influence of the external world" through conscious experience (Freud, 1923; rpt. 1961, p. 25). The superego is a part of the ego that is less firmly connected to consciousness and thus, for some purposes, it may be treated as a separate system. The superego, "the representative of our relation to our parents" and "heir of the Oedipus complex" (p. 36), was developed by the ego to resolve the sexual conflicts of the young child. Attached to both parents and sexually attracted in a special way by the parent of the opposite sex, the young child ultimately renounces this attraction. Identifying with the parent of the same sex, he or she attains a kind of substitute gratification. From this series of experiences the child incorporates the cultural ideals of its parents as guiding ideals, and comes to affirm them in a largely unconscious manner.

The process of "identification" provides for the internalization of social forces. In the words of Freud, "identification endeavors to mold a person's own ego after the fashion of the one that has been taken as a 'model'" (Freud, 1922, p. 63). The child creates within his psyche the forms experienced externally, thus in a psychological way he or she becomes these external objects. This is probably the central idea of Freud's specifically social psychology.

According to Freud, the most basic identifications are with parents. Very early, for example, a little boy will show special interest in his father and try to behave like him. Along with this identification with the father is a sexual tie to the mother. This Freud called a "sexual object-cathexis" (an attachment of libidinal drives toward an external object) rather than identification. For a while both of these ties to father and mother exist side by side, but they cannot be kept apart for long. Sooner or later the little boy recognizes that his father stands in the way of his desires for his mother. He then develops a hostility toward his father along with his love for the mother. This Oedipal situation (so termed by Freud because of its parallel to the life of the Greek tragic hero, Oedipus) is typically resolved by a strengthened identification with the father, and a transformation of his sexual interest in his mother into a form which is more socially acceptable. A corresponding resolution occurs for little girls as they strengthen their identification with their mothers. In either case, a set of ideals and inhibitions Freud called the superego becomes built up within the ego and influences all subsequent social interaction and self-evaluation. This superego may be formed with considerable variation in emphasis, depending on how the child resolves the crosscurrents of this situation of early conflict.

Later identifications are largely interpreted in terms of these earlier ones, for only these early ones, according to Freud, are structurally embodied in the superego. What may happen, however, is that many other figures may serve as substitutes for these primary identifications with parents. This is essentially what Freud saw as happening in the formation of social groups, as discussed in *Group Psychology and the Analysis of the Ego.*

In his analysis of group psychology, Freud took as his point of departure Gustave Le Bon's study of crowd behavior. He accepted Le Bon's analysis rather uncritically, for it served his purposes of seeing groups in their formative stages as rooted primarily in emotional ties. He then went on to specify the nature and origin of these ties. In a typical group, which has a clear leader and which is not particularly organized in a formal way, what has essentially happened is that the leader has temporarily become the common object of emotional orientation, substituting for the parental ties that formed the superego. And as group members use the leader to substitute for their superegos, they also have, in Freud's words, "identified themselves with one another in their ego" (p. 80).

To understand further features which he saw as characteristic of groups—"the weakness of intellectual ability, the lack of emotional restraint, the incapacity for moderation and delay, the inclination to exceed every limit in the expression of emotion and to work it off completely in the form of action" (pp.

81–82)—Freud found it useful to talk about a "herd instinct." Actually, he did not find it necessary to postulate such a tendency as genetically given. Instead he pointed to early rivalry between children and how the jealousy then felt is transformed into a common group feeling. This transformation is the basis for the esprit de corps of later groups and the standards of equality and fair play that develop through group life. Although Freud did not give a thorough theoretical discussion of this process, he did give a vivid illustration of what he had in mind. Note, said he, the way young women may gather around a pianist or singer after his performance. In one sense they are rivals for his attention; but "instead of pulling out one another's hair, they act as a united group, do homage to the hero of the occasion with their common actions, and would probably be glad to have a share of his flowing locks" (p. 87). In other words, they have successfully identified themselves with each other, allowing a common orientation to the object of their shared affections. This, suggested Freud, is basically what happens in most groups with effective leadership and favorable morale.

To supplement his interpretation of group processes in terms of parental substitutes and the transformation of childhood rivalries, Freud also sought in the history of the human species prototypes of characteristic events later observed in families. Earlier in *Totem and Taboo* he had presented a speculative treatment of events occurring in the "primal horde" (a conception of the original form of group life which he derived from the work of Charles Darwin), which set the stage for the formation of religion and standards of morality. In *Group Psychology and the Analysis of the Ego* he again took up the theme that present groups may also contain survivals of this primal horde. He speculated on the nature of the primal horde and how its characteristics were recreated in subsequent group life. The group leader, for example, always takes on something of the quality of the dreaded primal father, and the group still has a strong need for authority. In sum, said Freud, "the primal father is the group ideal, which governs the ego in place of the ego ideal"; that is, it carries on the conscience of long-past generations of group life in a manner analagous to the way individuals carry on the consciences of their parents in their superegos (pp. 99–100).

Despite his picture of the rather wildly irrational forces of group life, Freud also recognized that the individual is not just passively swept away by his group affiliations. He recognized how these affiliations became limited and differentiated for individuals involved. Each individual forms group ties in many directions, and these help to give a balance to his personality. Moreover, stable group affiliations form a basis for stability of personality. It is only in the rare occurrences of rapidly formed crowds that we sense the power of the group to play upon these inner forces, for here this power is relatively unchecked in its temporary expression. In fact, what we have in such temporary groups is something very similar to hypnosis, with the main difference being that crowd behavior involves identification with a whole set of fellow individuals as well as with a leader. In either case the apparently self-directed individual (in reality, the product of many, but well-balanced, social identifications) gives way to the dominating mastery of the immediate situation.

Society and Biology

In 1923 a cancer was discovered in Freud's mouth. An operation then arrested its development but left Freud unable to eat or speak without pain throughout the remaining years of his life. From then on he ate all his meals by himself, and he never gave another public lecture. Years later his cancer reappeared and, despite further surgery, led to his death on September 23, 1939. He died in London, England, where he had come the previous year as an exile from Hitler's *Anschluss* with Austria.

Despite his illness and pain, Freud remained a productive scholar almost to the end of his eighty-three years. In fact, his most notable contribution to the psychology of civilization, *Civilisation and Its Discontents,* appeared as late as 1930. The main theme of this work is the inevitable conflict between the demands of instinct and the requirements of civilization. "It is impossible," wrote Freud, "to overlook the extent to which civilization is built up upon a renunciation of instinct, how much it presupposes precisely the non-satisfaction (by suppression, repression or some other means?) of powerful instincts" (1930; rpt. 1961, p. 97). The two key examples are the impulses toward love and hate, central expressions of the basic instincts of life and death.

Freud saw two main forms of love: fully sensual or genital love, and "aim-inhibited" love or affection. Both of these become unavoidably opposed to the interests of civilization. Sexuality must be repressed to preserve family life. To Freud this repression was inevitable, but still somewhat extreme in its present extent. Freud was sure that men and women would be much happier with a less restrictive sexual code.

Simple affection (or aim-inhibited love) is also transformed by the forces of civilization to serve ends other than the happiness of individuals. For civilization "summons up aim-inhibited libido on the largest scale so as to strengthen the communal bond" (p. 109). Such processes of group identification had earlier been discussed in Freud's analysis of group psychology.

Another key motive is that of aggression. For Freud this was the most obvious manifestation of the death instinct.

Man's aggressive tendencies must of course be repulsed in the interests of building a civilization. This occurs not only in controls of antisocial actions, but it requires internal repression of aggressive impulses as well. As part of this process aggression is internalized and incorporated in the superego; there it turns inward as a feeling of guilt. In this way civilization "obtains mastery over the individual's dangerous desire for aggression by weakening and disarming it and by setting up an agency within him to watch over it, like a garrison in a conquered city" (pp. 123–24). Such guilt may be necessary for civilization to control aggression, but it is extremely damaging to the quest for personal happiness. Nevertheless, Freud considered such guilt as largely the inevitable by-product of cultural development. There appears to be no escape from the heavy burden of guilt civilization imposes upon us. We are therefore left "to find our way through tormenting uncertainty and with restless groping" (p. 133). In some individual cases where the strain is especially severe, psychoanalysis might provide some help. In following the formula Freud stated elsewhere for psychoanalytic treatment,* the ego might be strengthened to cope more effectively with this world of inevitable internal conflict. But the conflict still remains, for civilization requires it. For Freud, "the price we pay for our advance in civilization is a loss of happiness through the strengthening of the sense of guilt" (p. 124). This guilt is "to a large extent unconscious, appears as a sort of *malaise,* a dissatisfaction, for which people seek other motivations" (pp. 135–36). But it is nevertheless a very real part of our psychological natures.

In his closing comments of *Civilisation and Its Discontents*

---

* *"Its intention is, indeed, to strengthen the ego, to make it more independent of the superego, to widen its field of perception and enlarge its organization, so that it can appropriate fresh portions of the id" (Freud, 1933; rpt. 1964, p. 80).*

Freud saw some slight room for hope. Cultural development might possibly go in directions which were less directly repressive of individual happiness than that presently known. The antagonism between individual and society, though real, is not quite so fundamentally or biologically rooted as is the internal struggle between life and death forces. It is therefore at least conceivable that a more reasonable "cultural superego" might collectively organize our guilty consciences in the future. The concept of a cultural superego (or, as Freud also variously called it, the superego of the community or of an epoch of civilization) is an idea which Freud first presented in the closing pages of *Civilisation and Its Discontents*. He referred here to the ethical value systems of society, and set this collective superego off as analogous to, but distinct from, the superego of the individual. Freud offered an interesting parallel for cultural analysis here, but left such analysis undeveloped so far as his own work was concerned. It is in this direction that some of the psychoanalysts that followed Freud—especially "neo-Freudians" such as Abram Kardiner, Erich Fromm, and Karen Horney—extended psychoanalytic theory.

Throughout the development of psychoanalysis a central issue has always been the relative emphasis to be placed on biologically given forces in the interpretation of behavior. In its beginnings, psychoanalysis argued the case against the inflexible dictates of biological givens. Neuroses such as hysteria were not fundamentally determined by organic causes but were products of disturbed social experience. But, for Freud, the key to interpreting this disturbed experience must be found in the nature of inner forces which are themselves biologically determined. He thus took refuge in a theory of instincts—first especially libido, later the more generalized eros and thanatos—as the basis for mediating between biological determinants and social experience. Society may help give form to the expression of these impulses, but their basis—the basic impelling forces and their main directions of expression—derives from biological needs.

Freud's theory of instincts was probably the most controversial issue for debate within the psychoanalytic movement. It was primarily the interpretation of libido that led to the early breakaway schools of Alfred Adler and Carl Jung. Adler placed great emphasis upon a drive for power to overcome a feeling of inferiority. To him this, rather than sexuality, was the key to discovering the causes of neurotic symptoms. Jung, although he spoke of libido, extended the term to mean life energy in general. He gave greater emphasis than Freud to the "higher" motives, some of which he saw rooted in unconscious psychological processes just as surely as Freud saw there sexual and aggressive impulses. In part Freud's later theories took account of earlier objections of Adler and Jung. His stronger emphasis upon ego forces in his tripartite division of personality was at least in the same general direction as Adler's emphasis. And his broadening of the concept of libido in his revised instinct theory of eros and thanatos went in Jung's direction. But the split had already been established, and it continued.

Freud's theory of instincts was also a bone of contention with those later offshoots of psychoanalysis generally termed "neo-Freudian." Karen Horney, Erich Fromm, Harry Stack Sullivan, and Abram Kardiner had their differences of emphasis with each other, but all found Freud's instinct theories inadequate for handling the social variations of behavior. For them his theory was too narrowly formulated in terms of the individual, and the individual was too narrowly conceived of as driven by relatively fixed patterns of impulse. In contrast, they have contended that human beings are not born with fixed drives. As Clara Thompson (1950, p. 142) expressed this view, "Society is not something contrasted to man but something at the same time created by man and creating man." Society, in this view, is an ever-growing set of relationships that constantly changes the conditions for human behavior. Thus what Freud considered as inevitable conditions for early childhood socialization (for example, certain early family rivalries setting in motion the development of conscience) may in reality be much more open to variation. Indeed, perhaps most of his observations were based on a grossly unrepresentative sample of family life, using the rigidities and repressions of middle-class Viennese families during late-Victorian times as if they represented humanity in general. It may be, as Fromm has suggested, that some adjustment to the authority of parents is necessary in all societies, but this hardly requires the specific patterns of sexual repression and identification with parental substitutes Freud found most common among his patients. Rather, the neo-Freudians argued, we must be open to a greater plasticity of personality than Freud had perceived, reflecting the greater plasticity of society in which persons are formed.

The neo-Freudians have continued to use central ideas of Freudian psychoanalysis. They have generally assumed the centrality of unconscious emotional forces, the dynamics of repression and resistance, and the importance of childhood experience. They have also continued to practice Freud's key contributions to psychotherapy, especially free association, the interpretation of dreams, and the use of transference. But do these features of psychoanalysis really hold together without the uniting thread of a theory of instincts? A good number of Freudians today would say no. To leave aside the theory of instincts and the fundamental notion of organic tension reduction on which this theory is based is to set aside the very heart of psychoanalysis. In response, the revisionists (and with them most social psychologists) argue that Freud's individually centered and biologically based urges are inadequate as a basis for organizing social experience. The very nature of the human self may be more thoroughly social and cultural than Freud was able to conceptualize.

Perhaps, some revisionists feel, another way of formulating the central dynamics of social behavior would be more useful than that of using Freud; and maybe a beginning of this alternate way might be seen in the ideas of George Herbert Mead.

III

GEORGE H. MEAD AND SYMBOLIC INTERACTIONISM

Quiet Rebel

George Herbert Mead was born in 1863 in South Hadley, Massachusetts, where his father was a Congregational minister. Seven years later the Meads moved to Oberlin, Ohio, where the Rev. Hiram Mead became professor of homiletics at the Oberlin Theological Seminary. Not much has been recorded about the childhood of George Mead as he grew up in Massachusetts and Ohio, but he has been described as a "cautious, mild-mannered, kind-hearted, rather quiet boy" (Miller, 1973, p. xii). We do know that as a student at Oberlin College he experienced a sense of liberation from his early training, especially questioning the theological views with which he had grown up. But it was a relatively quiet and covert rebellion and created no stormy scenes with his parents. His father died in 1881, and his mother then took up teaching and later served for ten years as a college president at Mt. Holyoke College. There were no strained relations between the proud and dignified mother and her quiet son, though it is understood that they avoided discussion of sensitive philosophical issues. Meanwhile, George continued the gradual process of intellectual liberation, taking, he once said, his second twenty years to un-learn what he had been taught in his first twenty.

He formed a close friendship at Oberlin College with Henry Castle, who remained George's most intimate friend till his accidental death in 1893. After a break of four years after college, during which George unsuccessfully tried teaching grade school (he was fired after four months because of discipline problems) and more successfully served on a railroad survey-ing crew, Henry persuaded George to join him in studies at Harvard. There Mead became acquainted with William James; in fact, he lived in the James home and tutored their children. At the time, however, the psychology and philosophy of Wil-liam James did not make a strong impression on Mead. He was much more influenced by the lectures of Josiah Royce, who was then setting forth his interpretation of Hegelian ideal-ism. Here was the excitement of a new system of philosophy which was, as Mead later put it, "no longer the handmaid of theology, nor the textbook for a formal logic and puritan ethics" (quoted by Miller, 1973, p. xiv). Here was a free-flowing texture of ideas, opening the door to ever-broader questions about the nature of human experience.

After a year at Harvard, George Mead joined Henry Castle at Leipzig, Germany, where he also pursued his courtship of Henry's sister, Helen. George and Helen Mead were married in 1891, just before returning to the United States. By then George had taken up studies at the University of Berlin, con-centrating in physiological psychology. His friend Henry ex-plained this emphasis at the time as based on the desire to avoid religious controversy when he returned to America. "He thinks," wrote Castle, "it would be hard for him to get a chance to utter any ultimate philosophical opinions savoring of independence"; on the other hand, in physiological psychology he had found "harmless territory" (quoted by Miller, p. xvii). However, in 1891 when Mead received an invitation to return to the United States to teach in the University of Michigan's Department of Philosophy, he readily accepted. He left uncompleted the doctorate he was pursuing at Berlin, and he and his bride moved to a new home in Ann Arbor, Michigan.

It was at the University of Michigan that the general framework of Mead's philosophy began to take shape. The environment there seemed especially conducive. First of all, there was the recently named department head, John Dewey. Dewey, like Mead, had experienced Hegelian idealism as a liberating force, but both were now searching for more scientific foundations for philosophy. They saw the need for both a more biologically oriented and a more socially oriented base, and both men saw in the work of William James (whose *Principles of Psychology* had just been published) some important new leads for a science of mind. But neither Mead nor Dewey had yet clearly formulated his own position for philosophy or psychology.

Also at Michigan was a young man named Charles Cooley, who was then working on a Ph.D. in economics. Cooley was much impressed by some ideas he found in Adam Smith's writings regarding how persons must put themselves into the position of others in order to act effectively in society. The importance of this "sympathetic imagination" was later developed by Cooley in *Human Nature and the Social Order* as the idea of a "looking-glass self." Selves develop, according to Cooley, as they reflect the appraisals of others—an idea that Mead was to incorporate in his conception of role-taking. In fact, Mead was to push the idea farther than Cooley by raising questions about the origins of the mind, which Cooley assumed as given.

In the interaction of Dewey, Mead, and Cooley during their three years together at the University of Michigan, the main ingredients were being formed of a common orientation of the three toward social psychology. This common orientation was later to become called "symbolic interactionism," and Mead was to be—despite Dewey's greater general renown—its most authoritative spokesman. At the time, though, its principles still remained to be formulated and stated. George H. Mead was just beginning his career as a philosopher. He had resolved to forge his philosophy upon scientific foundations that would not take basic entities—such as soul or mind—for granted. Where exactly this would lead was not yet clear.

Chicago Philosopher

When William Rainey Harper was organizing the University of Chicago, he had three departments in mind to be given special strength: classics, Semitics, and philosophy. James Hayden Tufts, a philosopher and associate in Harper's organizing activities, made the suggestion that John Dewey head the philosophy department. When Dewey was offered the position, he agreed to come provided he could bring another young philosopher with him from the University of Michigan. And so it was that George H. Mead came to the University of Chicago in 1894 as Assistant Professor of Philosophy.

Under Dewey's leadership the new school was soon recognized as a center of the philosophical movement coming to be called "pragmatism." Tufts, Dewey, and Mead were all advocates of the approach in philosophy that saw the meaning of ideas identified by their practical consequences. After ten years Dewey left to go to Columbia, but Mead remained at Chicago for many more years. When he died in 1931 at the age of sixty-eight he was still professor of philosophy there.

During the almost forty years that Mead taught at Chicago, it remained a center of American pragmatism. John Dewey remained the intellectual leader of the group many years after he had left, but this was not simply a school of Dewey's disciples. A general orientation was shared, but each had his own area of special interest. Edward Scribner Ames had a particular interest in religion, as did James Hayden Tufts in ethics and aesthetics. Addison Moore focused especially on logic and epistemology. George H. Mead directed his attention especially to social psychology. And although John Dewey seemed interested in everything, he was particularly active in psychology and education. He founded Chicago's School of Education, and also presided over psychology within the Department of Philosophy.

Central in the philosophy of this Chicago school was a concern for process, for seeing ideas as a part of ongoing activity. All life is involved in activity, activity that takes place naturally and is organized by goals which themselves emerge and change through ongoing processes of adjustment and readjustment. Generally stated, this was the essence of the pragmatic philosophy which issued from Chicago.

Although John Dewey left Chicago in 1904, he and George Mead remained close friends throughout their lives. Mead, remaining at Chicago, eventually became chairman of the philosophy department himself, though he too had accepted an offer from Columbia shortly before his death. Mead generally recognized the leadership of Dewey and was never known publicly to criticize any of Dewey's ideas. Any reservations he expressed privately about Dewey's voluminous writings were quite minor; and on one occasion late in his life when asked if he really believed what Dewey had presented in *The Quest for Certainty,* his reply was "every word!" On his part Dewey acknowledged Mead's special influence in social psychology, where Mead's ideas "worked a revolution in my own thinking, though I was slow in grasping anything like its full implications" (Dewey, 1931, p. 313).

Mead is generally assumed to have had a special influence upon Dewey's 1896 paper, "The Reflex Arc Concept in Psychology." This paper set forth key ideas of what came to be known as the "functional" school of psychology and also serves a basis of criticism of much of the later behaviorist movement. The concepts of stimulus and response, then coming into psychology from physiology, were criticized by Dewey as artificial distinctions within an organism's ongoing process of action. The important features in this ongoing action are not specific parts of sensation, attention, and action, but the way the activity as a whole is organized and reconstituted in the ongoing adjustment of the individual. Instead of a disjointed psychology of distinct processes, Dewey was arguing for a more unified conception. The sensory stimulus thus becomes that phase of activity requiring definition and coordination, and it differs in part by the different definitions it receives. In a corresponding fashion the motor response is whatever completes the coordinated activity, and this too varies according to the definitions and purposes that direct the act. These larger functions of ongoing action must be recognized if sensory and motor activities are to be properly interpreted.

Mead himself did not publish any important articles in philosophy or psychology before the turn of the century, and throughout the rest of his life he only wrote about two dozen major articles. All of his books were published after his death, put together mostly from class notes by his students. His most complete manuscript was a series of lectures published in 1932 as *The Philosophy of the Present.* His social psychology lectures formed the basis of *Mind, Self and Society* (1934), and other lectures were compiled into *Movements of Thought in the Nineteenth Century* (1936) and *The Philosophy of the Act* (1938).

It was in the classroom rather than through the printed word that Mead had his primary impact, at least during his own lifetime. Still, his lectures were not very dramatic occasions. He seldom looked at his students, and he spoke with little expression. Looking at the ceiling or out a window, he sat and calmly lectured on the subject of the day.

Despite this rather distant style in the lecture hall, Mead made a profound impact on his students as he verbalized a philosophy well suited to the mood of the emerging social sciences in America—pioneering in spirit, scientific in method, and reformist in application. Chicago was the training center of many of the leading social scientists of America in the first half of the twentieth century. And the lectures of George H. Mead occupied an especially central place in the education of many of them.

Persons with informal contacts with Mead were frequently more impressed than were those who knew him as a teacher. He was a tall, handsome man of 200 pounds, physically active throughout his life. His interests ranged widely, including not only philosophy and social science, but also natural science, music, art, and literature. He is reported to have been able to quote John Milton by heart for as long as two hours, as well as extensive portions of Shakespeare, Wordsworth, and Keats. His many interests served him well as a conversationalist. His colleague Tufts called him "the most interesting conversationalist I knew" (quoted by Miller, 1973, p. xxxv). His students who saw him outside the classroom usually found him impressive as well. For example, one graduate student who came to Chicago about 1900 reported:

I took courses and seminars with Mead. I didn't understand him in the classroom, but for years Mead took a great interest in my animal experimentation, and many a Sunday he and I spent in the laboratory watching my rats and monkeys. On these comradely exhibitions and at his home I understood him. A kinder, finer man I never met (Watson, 1936, p. 274).

This student was to become the leading spokesman of American behaviorism, John B. Watson.

Mead's Social Behaviorism

In editing notes on Mead's classroom lectures for *Mind, Self, and Society,* Charles Morris picked up a phrase Mead had used rather incidentally. "Social behaviorism" is the tag Morris applied to emphasize both the social and naturalistic foundations of Mead's thought. Although this characterization is generally appropriate, we must clearly distinguish Mead's form of behaviorism from that (especially associated with John B. Watson) which became popular in psychological circles during Mead's later years. Watson's behaviorism had no place for "mind" or mentalistic concepts in the study of behavior. For Watsonian behaviorists, if psychology is to become scientific (and it must) it is necessary to abandon all concepts that cannot be observed externally. Although Watson and Mead were personal friends when Watson worked in the psychological laboratory in Chicago, Mead's brand of behaviorism was far removed from that of Watson's. For Mead mind was the central concern of psychological investigation, not to be proscribed because of its difficulty of objective measurement. But mental events were to be seen in terms of their behavioral context, and it is in this broader sense that Mead's social psychology may be considered as "behavioristic." In Mead's words,

Social psychology is behavioristic in the sense of starting off with an observable activity—the dynamic, on-going social process, and the social acts which are its component elements to be studied and analyzed scientifically. But it is not behavioristic in the sense of ignoring the inner experience of the individual—the inner phase of that process (Mead, 1934, p. 7).

What Watson and Mead had in common was a determination to take the behavioral context of events, rather than some independently existing mind, as the starting point for psychological investigation.

One particular feature generally associated with behaviorism—the tendency to reduce a phenomenon to its simplest units of behavior—was especially rejected by Mead. On the contrary, said Mead, "the behavior of an individual can be understood only in terms of the behavior of the whole social group of which he is a member" (Mead, 1934, p. 6), for it is this larger group that provides the context for individual acts. Mead's method was generally to proceed from the broader social forces to smaller events of individual behavior. In so doing he produced a psychology which, very much like the "functionalism" associated with Dewey, refused to limit attention to elementary units of behavior. Social acts were to be understood as entire processes, not as summations of particular stimuli and responses. As Mead expressed this point,

The social act is not explained by building it up out of stimulus plus response; it must be taken as a dynamic whole—as something going on—no part of which can be understood by itself—a complex organic process implied by each individual stimulus and response involved in it (Mead, 1934, p. 7).

Mead's conception of mental activity—his theory of "mind"—was based on an understanding of social gestures. In his analysis of gestures he drew particular inspiration from writings of Charles Darwin and Wilhelm Wundt.

Darwinism provided a general background for Mead's emphasis upon mind as emerging through processes of biological adjustment. In particular he saw in Darwin's *Expression of Emotions in Man and Animals* the basis for considering animal gestures as the starting point for the analysis of human language. Darwin had called attention to instances where initial parts of an act of one animal call forth modifications in the continuing response of another. For example, in a dog fight the acts of each dog become stimuli to modify the responses of one another. Darwin was interested in these gestures for their value in expressing inner emotions. Mead questioned the assumptions of Darwin's interpretation of social gestures, but he was much impressed by the significance of the acts to which Darwin had called attention.

Wundt had, according to Mead, seen more clearly than had Darwin the significance of the social gestures of animals. He saw that they did not so much express inner emotions as they reflected an external reality. They were parts of complex acts in which individuals responded to each other's acts. This led to seeing such gestures as parts of a social interaction rather than as expressions of individual sentiment. The social act involves two or more individuals, and their actions affect themselves and each other at one and the same time. Gestures are "those phases of the act which bring about the adjustment of the response of the other" (Mead, 1934, p. 45). Wundt, said Mead, had recognized how such gestures may serve as the starting point for self-consciousness. Following up on this lead was to be Mead's most distinctive contribution to social psychology.

As we approach human behavior from a general examina-

tion of animal gestures, we note an increasing amount of behavior not fully carried out. An act will be begun, but its
completion will be limited by greater inhibition and voluntary
control than is observed in lower animals. The gestures that
are given when acts are initiated, however, may carry some of
the meaning of the full act even though it is not completed.
Meaning arises from anticipated consequences, not from what
may actually happen later. "The feelings of readiness to take
up or read a book, to spring over a ditch, to hurl a stone, are
the stuff out of which arises a sense of the meaning of the
book, the ditch, the stone" (Mead, 1910, p. 399). Such an-
ticipations of ensuing action, when applied to social acts, may
carry meanings for all that are not fully realized by later actions. But the anticipation itself is the crucial thing—allowing
the creation through gestures (that is, through incipient parts
of an act) of that which may be associated with the full act. As
this becomes done more and more explicitly, we have the basis
of self-consciousness.

Some gestures are important because they represent the
same thing to all participants in a social act. These are especially susceptible to being shortened (allowing a simpler gesture to carry a fuller meaning) than is the case with other acts.
This allows one individual to put him or herself more easily in
the place of the other and sense the completion of the act being
represented. For Mead the vocal gesture was an especially important example. "The vocal gesture is of peculiar importance
because it reacts upon the individual who makes it in the same
fashion that it reacts upon another" (Mead, 1922, p. 160).
Such gestures can carry a great deal of shared meaning with
shorter and shorter forms, and they become increasingly used
in their abbreviated forms simply as carriers of this meaning.
They become what Mead called "significant symbols." Gestures become significant symbols when they arouse an implicit

response in their makers that matches the explicit response of others. "The individual's consciousness," in Mead's words, "depends on his thus taking the attitude of the other toward his own gestures" (Mead, 1934, p. 47). Such significant symbols become the foundation of language for human beings. They also become the stuff of human thought, for, according to Mead, mind or intelligence becomes possible only through this internalized conversation of gestures.

The meaning carried by significant symbols is always social in nature, for a symbol "always presupposes for its significance the social process of experience and behavior in which it arises" (Mead, 1934, p. 89). This "social process" is primarily a matter of human groups, groups which carry on action together and have come to share common significant symbols for carrying out this action.

Selfhood, according to Mead, grows out of the same conditions as those responsible for the development of "mind"—both being the emergence of significant symbols out of social acts. A self is any individual who is a social object to himself. To be a social object to himself means that the individual acquires meanings for his gestures similar to the meanings held by those around him.

Out of this capacity of an individual to take the role of other individuals toward himself develops what Mead calls the "generalized other." The generalized other is the organized set of attitudes that are common to a group, and that are taken on by the individual as a context for his own behavior. It is not enough simply to take on the role of particular others; the individual must also assume the attitude of the collective whole. This is essential for developing conscious organization in behavior, for "only in so far as he takes the attitudes of the organized social group to which he belongs . . . does he develop a complete self" (Mead, 1934, p. 155). And from the point of view of society, complex forms of human organization occur only by virtue of the ability of individuals involved to take the generalized attitudes of others.

The ability to organize the attitudes of others does not develop all at once. Its emergence can be identified in terms of two main stages of development. In the first stage "the individual's self is constituted simply by an organization of the particular attitudes of other individuals toward himself and toward one another in the specific social acts in which he participates" (1934, p. 158). This stage is sometimes called the "play" stage, suggesting a level of personal give and take. In contrast is the "game" stage when the attitudes of others become assimilated into a coherent generalized other. Then the "social or group attitudes are brought within the individual's field of direct experience, and are included as elements in the structure or constitution of his self" (p. 158).

To illustrate the notion of the generalized other and how it functions in the second stage of self-development, Mead points to a baseball team. The individual enters into the game only by taking on an entire structure of the expectations of others embodied in the rules of the game and the objectives of his team.

The game has a logic, so that such an organization of the self is rendered possible: there is a definite end to be obtained; the actions of the different individuals are all related to each other with reference to that end so that they do not conflict; . . . they are interrelated in a unitary, organic fashion (1934, pp. 158–59).

Out of such an incorporation of organized expectations emerges systematic personality organization. To continue with Mead's words:

The game is then an illustration of the situation out of which an organized personality arises. In so far as the child does take the attitudes of the other and allows that attitude of the other to determine the thing he is going to do with reference to a common end, he is becoming an organic member of society (p. 159).

Once fully developed, the self is nevertheless not static. It is always changing to the extent that an individual's group experience changes. But that is not the only basis of change in selfhood, as Mead makes clear in his distinction between the "me" and the "I" as two phases of the self. The "me" is the conventional and habitual organization of the self. It consists of the attitudes of others as organized into guides for one's own behavior. Because we incorporate these attitudes of others to form our own self-consciousness, the "me" is also the self-as-object we are conscious of when we reflect on our own behavior.

But if selfhood consisted only in the "me," our selves would simply be agents of society. Our only function would be to reflect the expectations of others. But there is more to the self than this, Mead insisted, even though such a "me" is that which we are most fully aware of in our own behavior. That something more Mead called the "I," referring to the active and impulsive aspects of the self. What we do when we respond to our image of self (the "me") is never exactly like that image. Something new is created between reflection and action, and that something new in action is Mead's "I." The "I" is thus the innovative and creative aspect of the self, allowing for new forms of behavior to emerge in action. Actions are not simply determined by the past, nor are they completely set by the self-conscious plans we hold as we begin an act. The acting part of the self, the "I," propels the action forward, generally, but never perfectly, in the routines envisaged by the "me" 's reflective self-consciousness.

The Mind in Action

Our discussion of Mead has emphasized the theme of ongoing action. This is the behavioristic side of Mead—that he traced significance to ongoing social behavior rather than to inward qualities of mind. For Mead the social act was the proper unit for social psychological analysis. An act, however, must be seen as including covert as well as overt aspects, for Mead was not a behaviorist if that term implies restricting attention to overt behavior.

The act, in Mead's analysis, typically has four phases, which can be identified as the "impulse," the "perceptual phase," "manipulation," and "consummation." The impulse sets an act in motion; the perceptual phase gives it direction; the manipulative phase provides execution; and consummation is the final experience that is brought by the act. For human beings the manipulative phase is especially important, for this is where we actually make contact with reality. And here Mead saw an especially crucial role for the human hand in the development of distinctively human nature. It is with the hand and its marvelous flexibility that we learn the various means that can be used to achieve our ends. And this awareness of various possible means adds enormously to the self-reflective character of human beings. Lower animals may have relatively little to separate the perceptual and consummatory stages of acts; however,

man's manual contacts, intermediate between the beginnings and ends of acts, provide a multitude of different ways of doing things, and thus invite alternative impulses to express themselves in the accomplishment of his acts, when obstacles and hindrances arise. Man's hands have served greatly to break up fixed instincts (Mead, 1934, p. 363).

Although the act can be analyzed as a unit of individual behavior, the content of a human act is typically a social content. It is social not just in the sense that it occurs in a setting involving more than one individual; it is also social in the more profound sense that the reflected judgments of others are woven into the act's initiation and execution. It is not just that other people are present around us that makes our acts social; much more important are the people who are present within us.

Other people are present within us through symbolic representation. The significant symbol that makes possible the self-consciousness and reflective action of human beings also brings with it the ingredients of language for the human community. It is through language that we as humans are able to possess fully reflective intelligence. And this language emerges—both for man at large in his cultural development and for the individual in particular in his life cycle—through a conversation of gestures with other individuals. It is thus through the development and use of significant symbols, first together with others and then only later within ourselves as thought, that we are the distinctive kinds of beings we are. This central importance of the societal and symbolic nature of human action has led to the common title of "symbolic interactionism" for the framework of social psychology, but it is also a more general philosophy of human nature.

The close continuity between the individual mind and society led Mead to apply a similar pragmatic philosophy to social action as to the action of the individual. Acts of individuals were seen as guided by social imagination, that is, socially based conceptions of what is likely to occur. Likewise, action in society is guided by an imaginative anticipation of what may be possible.

Mead himself was active in social reform circles in Chicago

and Illinois. A close friend of Jane Addams, he was associated with the settlement-house movement in general and with Chicago's Hull House in particular. He was also active in a variety of moves to further public education and to further the role of organized labor. Social reform seemed to him a natural way for a socially rooted mind to express itself in action. "It ought to be possible to . . ." was the phrase Mead's son remembered as most characteristic of his father's discussion of social problems (Dewey, 1931, p. 312), and with this recognition of the possible he would set out to consider how it might be accomplished. Such was the natural expression of Mead's pragmatic philosophy as applied to a world which was everchanging, but within which human values must be intelligently structured—and continually restructured. As Mead expressed this philosophy in *The Philosophy of the Act:*

We are all of us in some sense changing the social order in which we belong; our very living does it, and we ourselves change as we go on; there is always action to answer to reaction in the social world. That process of continuing reconstruction is the process of value, and the only essential imperative I can see is that this essential social process has got to go on. . . . It has to continue not so much because the happiness of all is worth more than the happiness of the individual but, being what we are, we have to continue being social beings, and society is essential to the individual just as the individual is essential to society (Mead, 1938, pp. 460–61).

Continuity

"More, I think, than any man I have ever known," John Dewey said about Mead, "his original nature and what he acquired and learned, were one and the same. . . . there was no division in his philosophy between doing, reflection, and feeling, because there was none in himself" (Dewey, 1931, pp. 310, 313). Such continuity of personality, especially the continuity of thought and action, apparently came more naturally for George H. Mead than for most philosophers. And this continuity also left its mark upon key themes in Mead's philosophy, including the continuity of action over time, the continuity of facts and values in action, and the continuity between the individual and society.

For Mead reality was always focused in the present, but the present included both a recognition of the past and a preparation for the future. The actions of men and women therefore always bridged these categories of time, anchored in an ongoing present.

Moreover, within Mead's pragmatic philosophy there was a continuity between facts and values. It is arbitrary to distinguish between what is objectively real, apart from any human purposes, and that which becomes involved in the realization of human ends. The former ("objective reality") is not factually perceived unless it relates to human values facilitating its perception; and the latter ("values") require a physical reality of some sort in order to carry any meaning.

The continuity of action over time and the continuity of facts and values were central themes in Mead's philosophy. But the continuity which was most specifically central in Mead's social psychology was the continuity between the individual and society. Individual selves require a society for their emergence and are created out of the stuff of social interaction. Society, too—though originally evolved before self-conscious minds—requires in its human form the conscious participation of individual men and women.

This continuity between the individual and society, along with a position of ultimate causal priority for society, made Mead's brand of social psychology especially popular among sociologists. And during Mead's last decade at Chicago his influence in its sociology department—itself the primary center then of American sociology—led to that department sometimes being called "an outpost of G. H. Mead" (Rucker, 1969, p. 22). Such men as W. I. Thomas, Robert Park, Ernest W. Burgess, Ellsworth Faris, and Louis Wirth (all leaders of American sociology and all at Chicago during this time) especially acknowledged their debt to Mead. For example, Faris, who became head of the sociology department in 1925, advised all advanced sociology students to take Mead's social psychology course, and most of them did.

Gradually the influence of Mead reached out beyond Chicago, and symbolic interactionism became the dominant theoretical theme among most sociologically trained social psychologists. There is no clearly defined school of orthodox Meadians, and it is usually impossible to identify exactly where symbolic interactionism extends when it is mixed with other interpretations. Nevertheless, it is possible to list a variety of overlapping lines of study that represent both the main lines of social psychological investigation among most sociologists and those areas especially influenced by the long shadow of G. H. Mead. Among these areas are role theory, reference-group theory, several variations of self theory, studies of occupational socialization, labeling theory in social deviance, the dramaturgical approach to social interaction, and ethnomethodology.

Most role theory uses role expectations as its central concept. There is a pattern of expectations of others identifying a person's role. How this is perceived by the individual largely determines his or her own behavior. Some role theorists focus upon groups and organizations, studying how different patterns of roles develop. Others focus upon individual behavior, often being especially interested in how conflict between different expectations may be resolved.

Many who have studied the influence of groups upon individuals have, with Mead, stressed the importance of how the individual *interprets* the group. This leads to the recognition that groups not physically present, perhaps even simple categories of persons with whom the individual compares his situation, may have an important impact upon his behavior. To identify the groups with reference to which a person behaves, and to study how such groups affect his attitudes and behavior, is the primary concern of reference group theory (or, as it is also often called, social comparison theory).

Self theory that follows the tradition of George H. Mead emphasizes the social content of the self. How the reflected judgments of others become organized into a pattern of self-evaluation is the central topic of attention. Empirical studies of self-conceptions usually include investigating how these are rooted in relationships to particular significant others.

Studies of occupational socialization frequently apply self theory and reference-group theory to a particular type of social context. Everett Hughes and his students have been especially active in this approach to studying a variety of occupations. Here the individual is seen as gradually acquiring a new set of meanings for his or her behavior to fit with the occupational setting, and how he or she learns these through interaction with others is a central concern.

The study of deviance has recently become a leading area for applying the interactionist perspective. How society labels certain actions as deviant is seen as the primary condition for deviance. How the individual responds to the judgments of others, including sometimes applying their labels to himself, is the other main concern in this "labeling" approach to understanding deviant behavior.

The dramaturgical approach to social interaction emphasizes the image of the world as stage. In this view, men and women constantly act for their audiences; how their "performances" are shaped by anticipated audience reactions is the main theme of this approach. Erving Goffman is especially prominent among sociologists who have applied this approach to a wide variety of social settings.

Ethnomethodology, as developed by Harold Garfinkel and others, is an approach that studies everyday social action from the actor's frame of reference. Emphasizing the individual actor's point of view, however, does not mean that all analysis must be limited to the awareness level of social actors. Rather this is a point of departure for examining those routine bases of social action usually carried out without much conscious reflection. Ethnomethodologists seek to clarify the social meanings of such action even when individuals involved may not be aware of these meanings. Like Mead, the ethnomethodologists see the meaning of an action rooted in ongoing social interaction.

Because Mead, unlike Freud, did not leave a clearly defined school of followers, there are a number of unresolved issues among those who follow in the traditions of symbolic interactionism. One of these is the basic nature of phenomena studied in social psychology. Another issue has to do with the nature of social causation. This concerns whether human behavior can be properly seen within a framework of antecedent causes. A third issue concerns the testability of the ideas of symbolic interactionism. Is it possible to formulate symbolic interactionist theory into testable hypotheses? To recognize some of the varieties of contemporary social psychology that follow from the work of G. H. Mead, let us briefly examine each one of these three issues.

What is the nature of the phenomena of social psychology?

To say, with Mead, that we must study "the behavior of the individual as it lies within the social process" (Mead, 1934, p. 6) does not help very much. It affirms that we should study the actions of individuals within a broader context, but it does not give us any firm handles for grasping that context. Some social psychologists use role theory to provide these handles, working with role expectations as the key for understanding patterns of ongoing social interaction. Others place the emphasis upon self-definitions that are continually restructured to apply to new situations. Still others insist that the ongoing action in its full social setting must be the focus of attention, often without being too clear just how this ongoing action is to be observed and conceptualized.

Insofar as social psychology is to be a science, our basic question becomes: What is to be observed? What are the key structures to focus on for empirical study? Mead himself does not give us much help here. He was a philosopher rather than a scientist, and his general emphasis was upon process, not structure. What then are the best tools for capturing the essence of the social process? There are no obvious answers here that have the consensus of symbolic interactionists. Some, such as Erving Goffman, simply observe the flow of behavior, taking careful note of the nature of the social setting in which it is structured and the changing definitions that become attached to the behavior. Others, such as Manford Kuhn, have given special attention to freely reported self-conceptions. Others, *symbolic* interactionists in a special sense, carefully observe language patterns. A few symbolic interactionists design laboratory experiments that attempt to capture some crucial relationship of social experience and self-conception; but most are skeptical about being able to capture the essential meaning of ongoing interaction within such an artificial framework.

The questions of the nature of phenomena leads directly to

matters of causal interpretation. Most science is based on a sorting out of possible causal influences of antecedent events upon subsequent events. But is this appropriate for human social behavior? Is human behavior to be understood as determined by antecedent causes? If we place emphasis upon the interpretive process through which a person constructs his or her acts, it may be misleading to identify antecedent events as causes of behavior. These have influence only because they are interpreted in a particular way, and they are interpreted in a particular way because of the purposes to which action is directed. Such considerations may well lead us to question whether any deterministic model is appropriate for application to human behavior. On this issue the tradition of symbolic interactionism is somewhat split. There are the indeterminists, led especially by Herbert Blumer, who emphasize that the creation of purposive behavior may involve using antecedent events—but only as interpreted within the ongoing construction of action. There are others who take inspiration from G. H. Mead who attempt to use conditions of social interaction as antecedent causes of self-conceptions or of subsequent behavior. Mead himself is nicely ambiguous on this issue. At some points his analysis suggests the indeterminism of a process of continual reconstruction of action, and at other points a sociological 'determinism seems to be the dominant theme. This is not necessarily a major inconsistency. If we consider determinism to be a relative matter (not an absolutely closed chain of causal forces such as Freud, for example, was willing to assume) then we can recognize certain types of antecedent events as most likely to be associated with subsequent behavior (including the internal processes of constructing that behavior). These might reasonably be called causes without necessarily implying that they produce effects separate from the interpretive process that organizes ongoing action.

Our difficulty in specifying what symbolic interactionists see as key observables and how they conceive of social causation should make us sensitive to the most general criticism leveled against symbolic interactionism in social psychological circles: that their ideas cannot be tested. But to mention such a criticism is perhaps to beg the question. Is it possible to formulate symbolic interactionist theory into testable hypotheses?

What George H. Mead has given social psychology is more of a general philosophical approach than a scientific theory. Furthermore, his emphasis upon ongoing interaction leaves the material for building scientific theory in something of a flux. Where are the clear phenomena, empirically measurable, that we can use to formulate testable propositions? We should not assume that symbolic interactionism is without such empirical propositions. For example, the following may be cited as propositions that have been empirically tested (and supported) in the area of self theory:

(1) The longer that persons occupy social positions, the greater are self-definitions influenced by such positions (Kuhn, 1960).

(2) Self-conceptions correspond more closely to perceived judgments of others than to their actual judgments (Miyamoto and Dornbusch, 1956; Quarantelli and Cooper, 1966).

(3) To the extent that other bases of evaluation are not available, an individual will come to expect behavior from himself in accordance with the evaluations he receives from others, especially from others perceived as more competent to judge and/or of higher general social status (Webster and Sobieszek, 1974).

(4) Stability of self-conceptions is greater with high consensus among significant others than when such consensus is lower (Backman, Secord, and Peirce, 1963).

Such propositions appear to reflect key predictions of symbolic interactionist theory, but they are also not very surprising. Would we really be able to imagine the reverse of any of these predictions? And if we should discover that the opposite pattern were true, couldn't this also be assimilated into a symbolic interaction perspective? For example, suppose we found that short-term social positions had a greater influence than long-term positions; could we not then suggest that a more recent position is more salient and thus more apt to be consciously drawn on in the construction of self-conscious action?

The conclusion that seems to follow from these considerations is that the central assumptions of George H. Mead and symbolic interaction are not themselves applicable to empirical testing. For example, how can we really test whether symbolic communication is essentially a product of social interaction? It seems sensible, but so does some genetic basis of language ability—and how can we separate the social from genetic components? Or how can we really test whether self-conceptions are necessarily mediated by linguistic cues? This too seems reasonable, but how can we prove it? Perhaps we cannot. Perhaps the only general test of symbolic interactionism is its pragmatic usefulness in organizing empirically relevant ideas about social behavior. And among those social psychologists who have a strong sociological background, the legacy of George H. Mead is especially likely to be valued in this pragmatic sense.

IV

KURT LEWIN
AND FIELD THEORY

Quasselstripper

In 1890, shortly after George Mead had begun his studies at the University of Berlin, Kurt Lewin was born in a small town in eastern Prussia. Twenty years later Lewin was himself at the same university, studying there, as had Mead, philosophy and psychology. In philosophy Lewin was particularly stimulated by the lectures of Ernst Cassirer, and in psychology he found a group of young psychologists at Carl Stumpf's Psychological Laboratory who had very exciting ideas. This is where the school of Gestalt psychology was about to emerge.

Lewin completed his studies at Berlin and entered the Kaiser's army just in time for World War I. In the war he fought at the front and was wounded in action. Recovering from his wounds on furlough, he married Maria Landsberg (a marriage which was to last scarcely a decade) and published his first psychological essays. After the war he returned to teach at the University of Berlin. This was the time that the school of Gestalt psychology was becoming a recognized group. Its leading spokesmen—Max Wertheimer, Kurt Koffka, and Wolfgang Kohler—were then all at Berlin's Psychological Laboratory.

The Gestaltists were in rebellion against psychological currents then dominant. It is not sufficient, they held, to identify the elementary sensations and associations involved in experience and assume that these can explain behavior. The important thing for the Gestaltists was the way experience is organized, not the elementary units in themselves. Their concern for processes of organization led the Gestaltists to emphasize the study of perception and to identify characteristic ways that perceptual processes are organized. We perceive, they held, according to patterns, and the process that patterns sensations takes precedence over the individual elements. Thus a melody will be perceived as one thing whether its elements are in the key of C or the key of G—two quite different sets of tones. Or a tree seen a quarter of a mile away will appear as approximately the same height as when seen at half that distance despite the differences in the angles at which the eye receives these different impressions. Proceeding beyond such general ideas, the Gestaltists designed experiments to identify the forces patterning perception and the characteristics of "good" perceptual organization toward which perceptions tend to be arranged.

Kurt Lewin became one of the Gestaltists, but he was never an orthodox follower of its early leaders. He did not emphasize the similarity in form of the organization of physical and psychological events, which was a doctrine of early Gestaltists. His interests were rather in the area of motivation than perception. And his work was directed more to questions of practical application than to understanding for its own sake. In all these respects Lewin differed from the main group of Gestalt psychologists.

Lewin's early published papers show a strong interest in applied psychology, especially concerning the effectiveness of agricultural and industrial workers. His interests in applied psychology and social reform continued throughout his life. At the same time, however, he was very much a theorist, deeply interested in the philosophy of science and attracted to mathematical abstractions. To him there was no sense of opposition between these practical and theoretical interests, for, as he is often quoted as saying, "there is nothing more practical than a good theory."

Lewin's methods as a teacher were unorthodox though effective. He did not lecture in the usual sense. Rather, he rambled freely, developing new ideas as he talked and welcoming contributions from members of the class. Using the blackboard frequently, he would try to give visual representation of his theoretical concepts.

In personal interaction with students, as in his teaching, Lewin was not highly organized. But he had an enthusiasm for psychological analysis that was contagious. This made his contacts with students strongly involving—so much so that sometimes afternoon student visitors to his home would become so occupied with discussion they would stay till after midnight.

Lewin seemed to be most effective when involved in informal group discussion. This led to the creation of a free-flowing, ongoing seminar of Lewin and his students every Saturday morning. Participation was open, and disagreement was freely expressed. The dominant atmosphere was that of an exciting search to break new ground in psychology. One student, Norman Maier, described these sessions as so characterized by a pioneering spirit that "It seemed as if all questions were being attacked from scratch" (Marrow, 1969, p. 24). There was a genuine give-and-take, with Lewin's ideas influenced by his students as well as the other way around. The close-knit group of students that developed as a result met regularly in a nearby cafe as well as at the Psychological Institute. At the cafe this group was called the *Quasselstrippe,* and the "ramblings on" (as the German name characterized their activities) would continue for hours. Usually about a half-dozen persons would be involved in a discussion that would change course from topic to topic, and then return to some key idea left hanging earlier. Lewin did not dominate the discussion, but he was the indispensable member, leading the discussion into new areas and assuring an enthusiastic hearing for creative new ideas.

One American student studying in Berlin, Donald MacKinnon, recalled a particular occasion that illustrates how the *Quasselstrippe* operated:

As is the custom in European cafes, you have a cup of coffee and talk and chat, then you order a piece of cake, more time goes by, some more cake, another cup of coffee, a process that may go on for two or three hours. On one such occasion, somebody called for the bill and the waiter knew just what everyone had ordered. Although he hadn't kept a written reckoning, he presented an exact tally to everyone when the bill was called for. About a half hour later Lewin called the waiter over and asked him to write the check again. The waiter was indignant. "I don't know any longer what you people ordered," he said. "You paid your bill" (Marrow, 1969, p. 27).

Lewin saw this as a dramatic illustration of the effects of tension systems, organized by goal-directed activities, upon the memory processes of individuals. Immediately the group began to discuss how this phenomenon could be studied through laboratory investigation, and the direct result was a doctoral dissertation by Bluma Zeigarnik, completed under Lewin's direction. The tendency to recall uncompleted tasks more readily than completed tasks became known as the "Zeigarnik effect" because of its demonstration in Zeigarnik's experimental study. This study seemed to confirm the fruitfulness of

Lewin's approach in seeing goal-oriented behavior as organized by tension systems that sustain the behavior until the goal is achieved and tension is released.

Other areas of investigation were similarly dealt with vigorously by Lewin and his students: the pursuit of substitute goals, determinants of level of aspiration, conditions for the arousal of anger, and the effects of need satisfaction are just a few areas where early studies were done. Gradually experiments on these subjects were reported by Lewin's students in the literature, and several of Lewin's own theoretical papers were widely read in psychological circles. By 1929, when he was invited to make a presentation to the International Congress of Psychology, he was beginning to be known to psychologists throughout the world. His approach, though generally considered within the Gestalt tradition, was also recognized as something new and original. "Field theory" was the name becoming attached to Lewin's new and original approach.

Lewin's Field Theory

In one of the most widely read of his German papers (included in *A Dynamic Theory of Personality*), Lewin contrasts the modes of scientific thought associated with Aristotle and Galileo. Aristotle's view of science was that its chief activity is to draw generalizations from a great number of similar cases. Some characteristic of its nature, in this view, determines whether one object is similar to another or different, and on the basis of these characteristics we classify the types of objects that produce different events. This leads to the conception of scientific laws based on repetition. To obtain a scientific law you need to establish similar results for a great number of similar cases.

In contrast, Lewin set forth the example of Galileo. To establish his law of falling bodies Galileo did not collect a lot of similar objects that naturally fell at the same rate. Galileo was not primarily concerned with simple appearances ("phenotypes," Lewin called them) but rather with the underlying, determining tendencies ("genotypes" to Lewin). These underlying tendencies showed that the speed of a fall was a direct function of time spent falling. True, feathers might *appear* to fall more slowly than iron balls, but only because air resistance is greater for them. Still, the essential dynamics of falling is the same for both and subject to the same underlying laws, said Lewin. To discover such laws it is not necessary to drop a great number of objects of similar characteristics. Just one falling object will be enough—provided it represents the true underlying dynamics.

Just as modern physical science has developed by abandoning an Aristotelian mode of thought for that of Galileo, so, proposed Lewin, psychology must also prepare for a similar transformation. Too much do we still see behavior as caused by the characteristics of the individual, he maintained. In this "Aristotelian" view, individuals behave the same way because of the similarity of their individual natures. But such a classification of behaviors by the characteristics of individuals, Lewin argued, will never lead us to valid scientific laws in psychology. What is needed is to get behind the appearances of behaving individuals to the truly determining forces of their behavior. And where may we find these truly determining forces? They must be found, Lewin asserted, through representing in some way the total psychological field of the individual. Only if we can represent the individual's total field of forces as they exist for him at a given point in time can we have the basis of precise prediction of his behavior.

In his concern to represent the total psychological field at a given time, Lewin felt it necessary to develop a new set of tools for conceptualization. For this he turned to topology, a nonquantitative mathematics of spacial relations. Lewin's use of topology was somewhat different from a mathematician's topology; for example, Lewin included positive and negative values in his representation of the segments of an individual's psychological field, though such assignment of values went beyond the limitations of traditional topology. Because he saw the events in an individual's field as goal-directed, that is, as organized in terms of some objective, he insisted on representing this in his diagrams of the psychological field. His topology thus became a kind of path space, expressing direction of movement as well as static relationships. To this use of topology he applied the term "hodological space."

Lewin's papers contain numerous illustrations of his use of topology. He would use an egg-like oval (or "Jordan curve," to use the mathematical term for an irregular, closed curving line) to identify the psychological field or "life space," separating it from the nonpsychological world. Within this oval would be marked off a number of regions to represent various aspects of current importance to the individual. One of these regions would ordinarily be identified as the present state or location of the person ("P"), and other regions would be marked with plus or minus signs to characterize their tendencies to attract or repel the person (what Lewin called "valence"). With such figures Lewin could map out what he considered to be the key features of the life space for a given individual at a given point in time. This assisted him in conceptualizing that what was happening was the product of a *field* of forces and was not simply caused by particular characteristics of individuals.

For his conception of a "field," Lewin drew on a definition of Albert Einstein. A field is "a totality of existing facts, which are conceived of as mutually dependent" (Mey, 1972, p. 22). The psychological experience of an individual consists of such mutually dependent facts and these can be thought of as constituting his "life space." The world as experienced by the individual at a given point in time is his life space, which always includes both the person and his psychological environment (that is, the environment as he perceives it at that time). Behavior is always a function of this life space, which in turn is always a product of the interaction between the person and his environment. In Lewin's field theory an act of behavior is never simply caused by the person or determined by factors of his environment. It is, instead, always a result of both acting upon one another.

The interplay of person and environment is always changing. Even though the life space includes events at only one point in time, it was important to Lewin to include in his representation of life space some indication of the direction of behavior. In his diagrams Lewin represented direction of movement within the life space by arrows, solid arrows for forces initiating movement and a broken arrow for the direction of change resulting from the various forces of movement.

Lewin did not provide clear specification of where to look for causes of change in the life space; this, he insisted, would have to come from the particular case being analyzed. In this sense his theory was a highly formal one that could be applied to almost any particular content. All he provided was the basic notion that the life space was in constant change, and that this change could be represented as a field of forces. The tendency of the person to change his location within the life space, that is, to move from one region to another (what Lewin called "locomotion"), is a result of this field of forces. The degree of attraction of various regions is represented by plus marks (or minus marks, in the case of repulsion) to indicate the "valence" of various regions. The valence of a given region is determined by the degree to which the various forces of the total field point toward it (or, with negative valence, away from it).

A tension system, in the broad way that Lewin used the term, represents any field in which behavior is directed toward some goal (that is, toward some region with high positive valence). This is typical of most behavior of interest to psychologists. Tension in this context simply means a readiness for action. Tensions may arise from some need within the person or from some feature of the environment (or, more often, from both together). Whatever the source of tension, the individual is set in motion, a motion that may be represented by the force-field arrows of his life space. Regions of his life space that are perceived of as likely to reduce the tension are the regions of strong positive valence (that is, goal regions). When an individual reaches a goal region the need initiating the movement may be satisfied, in which case the tension system is relaxed. If satisfaction is not realized, however, there may be a restructuring of the psychological field with another region serving as a new goal.

Simple tension systems simply produce goal-directed behavior. Frequently, however, the structure of the force field is such as to produce opposing tendencies of action. Lewin identified three main types of such conflict fields. The first type occurs when the individual is between two regions of positive valence. Then the problem is to choose between two goods. A second type of conflict occurs when the individual is between two regions of negative valence. Then, if he cannot restructure the field or leave it, he is faced with a choice between two evils. Finally, there is the type of conflict in which a possible direction of movement includes both positive and negative valences. Thus, a goal region may also carry negative effects, or a person may have to endure undesirable effects in order to reach the desired goal. Such conflicts are typical features of human action, and Lewin's "vector psychology" (that is, his conceptualization of fields of directed forces) provided a way to analyze such events.

In order to understand the behavior of an individual, Lewin insisted, we must know the totality of forces operating in his psychological field. It is the total field, not the elements in isolation, that produces his behavior. This behavior, moreover, always takes place in the present. Therefore Lewin saw no need to include past events in analysis except insofar as they were a part of the present psychological field. That is, only to the extent that a past event was still a part of the psychological experience of the individual could it be a determinant of his behavior. Or so at least was assumed by Lewin's field theory.

Field theory, as we have outlined its main ideas, is a way of looking at behavior rather than a set of substantive assertions about particular forms of behavior. That this way of viewing behavior may bear fruit when applied to more concrete issues may be illustrated by reference to several areas explored by Lewin and his students. We might mention in particular the selective recall of unfinished tasks, the substitute value of alternative activities, studies of satiation, and level of aspiration.

When behavior is directed toward achievement of a goal, attention is sharpened. Once a goal is reached, however, attention becomes more relaxed. This implication of Lewin's analysis of tension systems led Bluma Zeigarnik to predict that unfinished tasks would be recalled more accurately and fully than would completed tasks. Her experimental demonstration of this—the so-called "Zeigarnik effect"—led to further analysis of the relative strength of motives in achieving goals. When the same degree of influence is used to seek recall of different tasks, those that show a higher "Zeigarnik quotient" (the ratio of unfinished tasks recalled to completed tasks recalled) can be inferred to be more strongly motivated. An exception to this tendency of the Zeigarnik effect occurs when not completing a task may be interpreted as a personal failure. Then an additional force acting against recall of uncompleted tasks may be included, sometimes reducing the Zeigarnik quotient to below 1 (that is, leaving the completed tasks better remembered).

Techniques similar to those used by Zeigarnik in studies of memory were applied by other students of Lewin to analyze the phenomenon of "substitute value." When an activity is interrupted and another activity is then pursued, some of the tension associated with the first activity may be carried over to the second. The second activity may therefore be said to have substitute value. How much substitute value it has may be indicated by certain experimental techniques. When the substitute activity is completed, its value as a substitute may be indicated by the strength of the tendency to resume the original activity. If there is little substitute value, there is a greater tendency to resume the original activity. Thus the increase or decrease in the tendency to recall the original task may be used as an index of substitute value. Studies using such techniques have yielded a number of important generalizations about the substitute value of activities. For example, the more similar and the closer together in time are two activities, the more substitute value will the second have for the original activity. Also, the more attractive a new activity, the greater will be its substitute value.

Continued activity within a goal region may lead from a positive to a negative valence for that region. This is more popularly expressed in the concept of satiation. Lewin and his students have pointed out that the way satiation occurs depends upon the way particular needs are embedded in a tension system. Satiation occurs more slowly in a large or complex system than when a simpler set of actions are involved. Also, the more central the activity for a person, the more quickly may satiation be realized.

Goals toward which a person strives may have different degrees of difficulty. This idea is the core of the concept of level of aspiration. Sometimes attention may be directed toward goals that are easier, and sometimes toward those that are more difficult. Lewin and his associates developed a theory to predict the degree of difficulty that will be selected by an individual. According to their theory, the valence of any level of difficulty is a function of the combined effects of the valence of achieving success, the subjective probability of success, the valence of possible failure, and the subjective probability of failure. Experimental work by students of Lewin then and now has focused upon each of these factors of level of aspiration as well as the way they are combined in serving as a basis of behavior.

Lewin's genius was especially seen in his combination of formal theory with questions of vital psychological interest. This can only be roughly perceived from the examples we have just sketched. But they at least express the directions in which his field theory was applied in his early work at the University of Berlin.

New Directions

As Kurt Lewin grew up in the village of Mogilno, now part of Poland but then in Prussia, he was quite aware that Jews were considered somehow different from most Germans. His father owned and operated a general store, above which the family lived, and he was active in local affairs. But it was clear that as Jews the Lewins could never move in higher social circles, given the prevailing anti-Semitism.

At the University of Berlin Lewin received respect and recognition despite his Jewish background. But this suddenly changed in the early 1930s. In 1932 Lewin was invited to Stanford University in the United States for a brief period as visiting professor. While Lewin was returning to Germany early the next year, Adolf Hitler became Chancellor of Germany. As a Jew, Lewin quickly realized that he had little future in Germany, and he immediately sought a job in the United States. Later in 1933 he moved with his new wife Gertrud and their young child (he had been remarried in 1929) to Cornell University, where he had a two-year appointment at the School of Home Economics. The position was only a temporary one, supported by foundation funds. Later he moved to the University of Iowa (from 1935 to 1944) and finally to the Massachusetts Institute of Technology, where he established the Research Center for Group Dynamics (just two years before his death in 1947 from a sudden heart attack).

In the United States Lewin's theoretical ideas matured. His first book, *A Dynamic Theory of Personality,* an English translation of earlier German articles, appeared in 1935; and the next year his *Principles of Topological Psychology* was published. Among other theoretical writings of Lewin, the most important are contained in *Field Theory in Social Science* (1951), a posthumously published collection edited by Dorwin Cartwright, Lewin's successor as Director of the Research Center for Group Dynamics when it relocated at the University of Michigan.

The United States offered special opportunities for Lewin's

desire to do research oriented to practical problems. He was constantly involved in one form or another of research concerned with social problems, whether working with Margaret Mead and the National Research Council to discover the best way to change food habits during World War II; or analyzing the effects of group participation in decision making upon the productivity of the Harwood Manufacturing Corporation; or evaluating psychological warfare activities of the Office of Strategic Services in Washington. This penchant for research geared toward social action (or, as he called it, "action research") led Lewin to establish two new important research organizations during the last years of his life. During 1944 and 1945 Lewin was busy founding at the same time the Research Center for Group Dynamics at the Massachusetts Institute of Technology and the Commission on Community Interrelations of the American Jewish Congress in New York. The latter organization was especially active in studying the causes of intergroup tensions and how prejudice and discrimination may best be attacked.

Personal tragedy and dramatic world events underlined Lewin's interest in social action, especially that geared to improved intergroup relations. His mother was still living in eastern Germany as war clouds of World War II gathered. Working desperately to get her out, he tried every diplomatic avenue available, without success. Sometime during 1943 or 1944 she died at a Nazi extermination camp in Poland.

During his last few years Kurt Lewin gave special emphasis to projects designed to attack prejudice and improve intergroup harmony. Urging legal action against discrimination as a means of attacking prejudice, studying racial integration in housing or work groups, and analyzing the best means of confronting bigoted attitudes are a few of the activities that occupied Lewin most in his final years.

In all his works—developing theory, testing theoretical ideas experimentally, or promoting action research—Lewin was constantly talking with those in his group. There was always a circle of enthusiasts who formed around him. In America, Berlin's *Quasselstrippe* became transformed into Iowa City's "Hot-air club," which met regularly at a place named the Round Window Restaurant. Associations of staff members at the Research Center for Group Dynamics and the Commission on Community Interrelationships had much the same character during Lewin's last years. It is remarkable how many of Lewin's students and close associates have gone on to become leaders in American social psychology. There was Fritz Heider, fellow refugee from Germany, first recognized in America as a translator of Lewin's *Principles of Topological Psychology*. There were his Iowa students such as Roger Barker, Alex Bavelas, Dorwin Cartwright, Leon Festinger, John R. P. French, Jr., Ronald Lippitt, Ralph White, Herbert Wright and Alvin Zander—all of whom later made distinctive contributions on their own. Other social psychologists who first gained recognition through Lewin's Research Center for Group Dynamics were Kurt Back, Morton Deutsch, Harold H. Kelley, Albert Pepitone, Stanley Schachter, and John Thibaut. Together these names constitute at least half of America's most prominent social psychologists of the 1950s and 1960s.

Lewin's Group Dynamics

Kurt Lewin was in his element with an informal seminar group. He was not at his best in a formal lecture, but in a freely interacting group he came into his own. This was not only his habitual style of operating, but it expressed as well a key element in his personal belief system. He had a profound faith in democracy, which to him was much more than just a political system. It was also a way of life, based on mutual participation and continual interaction in decision making. On this particular issue Lewin would sometimes become a bit overbearing; as his onetime colleague Robert Sears once commented, "The autocratic way he insisted on democracy was a little spectacular" (quoted by Marrow, 1969, p. 127).

Given this concern for democratic decision making, his interest in social action, and his own style of working with groups, it is not surprising that Kurt Lewin turned increasingly in his years in America to the study of group dynamics.

Lewin's field theory provides a natural theoretical base for an interest in group action. The inclusion of the environment within the concept of life space provides an avenue for the incorporation of group concepts. The functioning of particular groups can thus be seen as chief parts of the life space for most individuals. It is therefore a small step from the study of the life space of individuals to that of group influences upon behavior.

In studying group influences upon behavior, Lewin felt it important to distinguish between "own" and "induced" forces toward changes in life space. "Own" forces are those that stem from the needs of the person himself, while "induced" forces come from part of the surrounding environment. The most effective influences toward social change, Lewin insisted, were those that would involve the "own" forces of individuals as well as the inducements found in the various "power fields" affecting him from without.

Although such a distinction as has just been made between "own" and "induced" forces is vital for understanding changes, we must be careful not to identify group behavior simply with the "induced" category. A group is not necessarily external to the individual, for to conceive of groups in such a way would contradict the central assumption of field theory. The behavior of a group, just as the behavior of an individual, is based on a set of interdependent facts; and it is the interdependence of these facts that constitutes the nature of group behavior. A group is therefore not basically a collection of individuals; it is rather a set of relationships involving individuals. It is the interdependence found in these relationships that constitutes the group, not the characteristics of individual members.

This view of the nature of groups allows us to see group actions varying in the degree to which they involve "own" forces of individuals. Usually, however, an established group includes strong links with the motives of individual members such that there is no clear separation between group goals and purposes of its individual members. It is for this reason that it is generally easier to induce social change by involving groups rather than through individuals directly. To use Lewin's words:

. . . experience in leadership training, in changing of food habits, work production, criminality, alcoholism, prejudices—all seem to indicate that it is easier to change individuals formed into a group than to change any of them separately. As long as group values are unchanged the individual will resist changes more strongly the further he is to depart from group standards. If the group standard itself is changed, the resistance which is due to the relation between individual and group is eliminated (Lewin, 1951, p. 228).

Lewin's own work during World War II involving attempts to change food habits seems to give direct support to these conclusions. A process of group discussion and group decision proved far more successful in inducing housewives to increase milk consumption than did individual appeals through lectures. Similar results were found with other groups of mothers who were informed of the virtues of orange juice and cod liver oil for their babies. Such studies suggested to Lewin new insights more generally applicable to social engineering. He came to talk a great deal about planned social change, which he saw as best engineered in three phases. First was "unfreezing," or reducing the relevance of past group standards; next was the introduction of new standards; and finally was a "refreezing" process, which firmly established the new standards. In all of these phases involvement of the individual in a group decision was more likely to bring about change than would an appeal to him or her as an individual. Individuals are more willing to consider new standards if their group explicitly reduces the relevance of past standards (which sometimes requires a new setting, such as a weekend workshop). New standards are more likely to be accepted if they are seen as being decided by the group rather than as imposed from without, and they will be assimilated more naturally if a group is involved in the follow-up.

Sometimes Lewin was concerned to show a continuity between studying the life space of individuals and studying the dynamics of groups. He indicated at one point a method for charting a social field based on the combined life spaces of the individuals involved. He also recognized, however, that this procedure would be enormously difficult if extended to groups of more than two or three persons over any significant span of time. For the most part Lewin was content to analyze group phenomena without attempting to represent groups in terms of individual life space. Sometimes he spoke of the life space of the group, thus applying to a group the same kind of field-theory analysis as would apply to individuals.

The most famous group study inspired by Lewin was the research on social climates of groups carried out in 1938 and 1939 at Iowa City by Ronald Lippitt and Ralph White. They set up a number of children's play groups with different styles of adult leadership. The first set of studies compared the results of autocratic and democratic patterns of leadership. A second set included these two styles plus a "laissez-faire" variation, a kind of nonleading "leadership," to compare with leader-centered ("autocracy") and group-centered ("democracy") styles. Detailed observations, including counts of different kinds of actions and notes on group effects, were made for all groups. Each group of children experienced more than one leadership style so that change could be studied as well as comparisons made of different styles for the same group. The results of these studies have been frequently cited to show the advantages of democracy over autocracy. Under autocratic leadership, for example, there was less initiative and more aggression against fellow members than in other treatments. Democratically led groups were best in these respects, and also were clearly preferred by most members. Laissez-faire groups showed a general aimlessness and discontent which also was not characteristic of democracy.

The Iowa studies of group leadership and social climates reflect Lewin's conviction that procedures of experimental psychology can be systematically applied at the group level of analysis. The results also appear to reflect Lewin's profound faith in the virtues of democracy. "Social action through group action" is one of the strongest themes running through the more applied work of Lewin, and the group action he envisaged was one that involved to a high degree as many of the individuals concerned as possible.

This emphasis upon groups and the necessity of strong involvement of individuals for group action led to a direct link between Lewin's work and the sensitivity training movement that has developed in the years since his death. In fact, Lewin might in a real sense be called the father of sensitivity training (or perhaps its mid-wife) because of his role in the origin of what have since been termed "T-groups." The year before his death Lewin was approached by the Connecticut State Interracial Commission to help set up some training sessions for its staff. This was done in a two-week program during June, 1946. During one evening session Lewin's research staff met to discuss their observations of the day; when some of the trainees asked for permission to sit in on these sessions, the nature of these sessions became transformed. Alfred Marrow (1969, p. 212) decribed these events as follows:

> Most of the staff feared that it would be harmful to have the trainees sit in while their behavior was being discussed. Lewin, however, saw no reason why the researchers should keep data to themselves, nor why feedback to the trainees should not be helpful. The result—in the words of Bradford—was like a "tremendous electric charge . . . as people reacted to data about their own behavior."

Lewin led the workshop to incorporate both observer feedback and self-analysis of behavior into its practices. Building upon this experience, he set about founding a new organization, the National Training Laboratories, to be centered at Bethel, Maine. Before the first session of this new organization, however, Kurt Lewin was dead. Among his last efforts was bringing to birth the organization that was to make T-groups (groups led by a relatively nondirective but sensitively observing "trainer") a significant part of the sensitivity-training movement in the 1960s and 1970s.

The Eternal Present

For his friends Lewin's tardiness was one of his most exasperating characteristics. He seemed oblivious to scheduled time in pursuing his interest of the moment, and as a result was habitually late for appointments. Perhaps we should take care in generalizing from such a personal idiosyncrasy, but there is at least a parallel to be made between Lewin's personal attitude toward time and that of his general theoretical approach. Field theory, like Lewin himself, seems oblivious of time. There is only the eternal present. And also, again like Lewin himself, this eternal present is never a closed product, but always appears to be seeking out new possibilities.

Its ahistorical character is one of the most notable features of field theory. The person is seen as constantly preparing to act. The past is relevant only as it is a part of the present field of forces. The future is important only as it organizes the goals pursued in the present. With this limited time frame—"postperceptual and prebehavioral," as it has been characterized by another psychologist—it is almost impossible to derive directly any predictions. We never know all that is really going into the psychological field or what forces might be changing it from moment to moment. And because the framework is focused at a given point in time, we do not have a good basis for analyzing the relationship between antecedent conditions and subsequent events.

A similar ahistorical character marks much of the more specific work of Lewin and his followers. In group dynamics, for instance, the emphasis was upon how present situational events may change the flow of behavior in groups. This led to an emphasis upon how situational events as perceived by participants shape behavior in groups. With this emphasis upon the here and now (and a lesser concern with long-term personality dispositions or large-scale institutional structures of society) it becomes more reasonable to see a major outgrowth of Lewin's group dynamics in the sensitivity-training movement.

Though somewhat broken off from past determinants, the present in Lewinian theory is systematically future-oriented. Life space seems constantly organized around what might become, what the individual (or group) is trying to achieve. This gives a purposive character to field theory, but the purposes are never rigid or fixed. They are themselves influenced by the flow of events in the present and by changing perceptions of what might be.

Because of these ahistorical and purposive features, Lewinian theory has a somewhat mixed scientific character. On the one hand, Lewin inspired rigorous scientific procedures. He was a leader in the development of experimental techniques in social psychology. At the same time, there is a kind of subjectivity about field theory. There is never certainty about exactly what is part of the field and what is not, nor is there any clear way of measuring the main components of a field. By default, then, Lewin's field theory leads us into phenomenology. Since we are given no clear criterion to identify what is important in the set of interdependent facts of the total situation for an individual, we tend to accept whatever that individual sees as important. And that is essentially the way Lewin usually applied his concept of life space. Behavior was essentially seen as determined by those facts the behaving individual consciously considers to be important. At times Lewin seemed to stop just short of a phenomonological position; there are, after all, some facts that may affect parts of the field without a person's conscious awareness. And Lewin did recognize such forces under the concept of "psychological ecology." But generally these were secondary considerations. The prime task of the psychologist, what Lewin specifically defined as psychological "objectivity," was to represent the field "correctly as it exists for the individual in question at that particular time"

(Lewin, 1951, p. 240). And this involved analyzing behavior from the perspective of the person involved.

Whatever its status as science, Lewinian field theory proved enormously productive for organizing ideas of the emerging field of social psychology. His emphasis upon organization of forces was nicely congruent with some of the main emphases of social psychology in the decades since his death. For example, much work in the area of attitudes has been organized in terms of one or another form of consistency theory (emphasizing how attitude elements are associated together in a field), and it is perhaps more than a coincidence that the two most prominent forms, balance theory and dissonance theory, were first formulated by close associates of Lewin (Fritz Heider and Leon Festinger, respectively).

Furthermore, Lewin's insistence upon examining behavior as a field of forces and not as a set of isolated events built social psychology more naturally into general psychology than was possible for any other system. This led to the ready conceptualization of social facts as central ingredients in individual behavior. The same system, moreover, could readily be applied to groups as systems of behavior in their own right. In the study of groups, Lewin's associates in the Research Center for Group Dynamics have continued to lead the way for other social psychologists.

Lewin's skill at experimental formulation was another chief reason for the productivity of his system. He had a genius for thinking of ways to apply ideas experimentally, and he inspired in his students something of this ability for experimental imagination. This came at a time when social psychology was becoming especially conscious of the need to demonstrate its assertions through experimental evidence. Much of the work of Lewin and his students would be impressive as experimental work even if it had not been formulated in the language of field theory.

Another strong feature to help explain Lewin's enormous influence was his sense of the need to combine theoretical research and practical affairs. He was a doer, and he wanted research that made a difference in the real world of human affairs. This fit very much with the temper of much American social science in the 1930s and 1940s (and since), and it probably helps to explain why his influence was and still is so substantial. He was constantly suggesting ways to bridge the gap between theoretical social science and public policies and practices. And the particular content of the applications he suggested were very much in the American grain, especially during the time he lived in the United States. It was a time of social change and reconstruction in the name of those democratic values most dear to Kurt Lewin (shared participation in purposive change). No matter that much of the past might be forgotten in the process; for Lewin the only important factors were those that effectively activate human beings at the particular time they are living.

V

B. F. SKINNER AND OPERANT BEHAVIORISM

Psychological Technologist

Burrhus Frederick Skinner was born on March 20, 1904, in Susquehanna, Pennsylvania, the son of a small-town lawyer. He had a generally pleasant childhood among the hills of eastern Pennsylvania, which he has recorded in detail in a recent autobiography (Skinner, 1976).

One special characteristic of his early life that was to foreshadow later events was his penchant for invention. As he later recalled in a brief autobiographical account:

I was always building things. I built roller-skate scooters, steerable wagons, sleds, and rafts to be poled about on shallow ponds. I made see-saws, merry-go-rounds, and slides. I made slingshots, bows and arrows, blow guns and waterpistols from lengths of bamboo, and from a discarded water boiler a steam cannon with which I could shoot plugs of potato and carrot over the houses of our neighbors. I made tops, diabolos, model airplanes driven by twisted rubber bands, box kites, and tin propellers which could be sent high into the air with a spool-and-string spinner. I tried again and again to make a glider in which I myself might fly. . . . I used to gather elderberries and sell them from door to door, and I built a flotation system which separated ripe from green berries. I worked for years on the design of a perpetual motion machine. (It did not work.) (Skinner, 1967, p. 388)

Skinner studied at Hamilton College in Clinton, New York, where his major field was English literature. He took no courses in psychology, but did win a special award for his work in Greek. He was also elected to Phi Beta Kappa, an organization which he, a campus rebel, had publicly attacked. During his senior year he sent some of his short stories to the poet, Robert Frost, whose response was very encouraging. After college he spent some time writing fiction, but he soon gave up on that venture. As he later explained, "I discovered the unhappy fact that I had nothing to say, and went on to graduate study in psychology, hoping to remedy that short-coming" (quoted in *Current Biography,* 1964, p. 421).

Meanwhile, Skinner's appetite had been whetted for behaviorism. He credits Bertrand Russell with his first introduction to it. Russell published a series of articles in *Dial* magazine on the behaviorism of John B. Watson, which the young Skinner read. Years later Skinner told Lord Russell of this introduction to behaviorism. "Good Heavens!" was Russell's reply, "I had always supposed that those articles had demolished Behaviorism!" (Skinner, 1972, p. 103).

But at least Russell had taken Watson's behaviorism seriously. Watson, who was then the leading spokesman for behaviorism in psychology, identified psychology as the objective study of behavior. In Watson's view, there was no room for mentalistic concepts; all subjective concepts were to be replaced by physical indicators of stimulus and response. As he had expressed the proper goal for psychology in his *Psychology from the Standpoint of a Behaviorist* in 1919, it was the "ascertaining of such data and laws that, given the stimulus, psychology can predict what the response will be; or, on the other hand, given the response, it can specify the nature of the effective stimulus" (Watson, 1919, p. 10).

Although Watsonian behaviorism was not dominant at Harvard, where Skinner went for graduate work in 1928, it had become sufficiently respectable that he had little difficulty in charting his graduate career by its guidelines. In three years he was awarded the Ph.D., writing a doctoral dissertation that attempted to specify behavioral laws for operations of the central nervous system.

Remaining at Harvard for five years after his degree, Skinner carried out research designed to identify basic laws in the behavior of organisms. In the process of studying rats in his laboratory, he made a number of important changes in the apparatus used. One was to arrange for the automatic recording of behavior on a moving paper tape. Another change was to arrange for the animal in the apparatus to operate the mechanism that would deliver the reward. This was most commonly done by pressing a bar or some other simple lever. By combining these innovations, bar-pressing responses could automatically be recorded to indicate the frequency of a simple response representing the organism as a whole. Thus was born the "Skinner box," which has since become one of the most common tools of psychological research. Skinner used it to investigate the effects of different schedules of reinforcement upon lever-pushing behavior.

According to Skinner (1972, pp. 110–11), his interest in schedules of reinforcement was partly the result of accidental circumstances. One Saturday he noticed that he would not have enough food pellets to last through the weekend. So he changed his system so that no more than one response would be rewarded for each minute. This way he had plenty of pellets. He also found his rats stabilizing their behavior at a steady pace. He then went on to study the effects of different kinds of partial reinforcement, at variable or fixed ratios to the amount of lever pressing. The results showed characteristically different response patterns, and the effects of such different contingencies of reinforcement were a central part of the subject matter of Skinner's first book, *The Behavior of Organisms* (1938).

By the time his first book was published, Skinner had left Harvard to teach at the University of Minnesota. He was there as World War II approached, and in 1940 was involved in a project with considerable potential for the war effort. His project was, in brief, to demonstrate that pigeons could be trained to direct a guided missile to its target. As he later described an early test:

The pigeon, held in a jacket and harnessed to a block, was immobilized except for its neck and head. It could eat grain from a dish and operate a control system by moving its head in appropriate directions. Movement of the head operated the motors of the hoist. The bird could ascend by lifting its head, descend by lowering it, and travel from side to side by moving appropriately. The whole system, mounted on wheels, was pushed across a room toward a bull's eye on the far wall. During the approach the pigeon raised or lowered itself and moved from side to side in such a way as to reach the wall in position to eat grain from the center of the bull's eye. The pigeon learned to reach any target within reach of the hoist, no matter what the starting position and during fairly rapid approaches (Skinner, 1960, pp. 28–29).

Later improvements simulated placement of the pigeon inside an air-to-ground missile warhead, pecking at a plate to control the descent of the bomb. Its pecking was to be guided by visual patterns representing fields of radiation—the same kind of information available to a human bombardier. The initial stage of the project was federally funded by a grant to General Mills, which had earlier been persuaded to sponsor the project. However, it was never put into effect. In 1944 Skinner's group was given a final opportunity to demonstrate the feasibility of the project to a committee of leading scientists. They brought a pigeon along to perform for the scientists, and it did perfectly. "But," as Skinner later recalled, "the spectacle of a living pigeon carrying out its assignment, no matter how beautifully, simply reminded the committee of how utterly fantastic our proposal was" (Skinner, 1960, p. 34). The project was not funded any further. Nevertheless, Skinner believes that subsequent research by the Navy has proved that the project was feasible in its basic outline. It is, at any rate, no longer the "crackpot idea" it seemed during World War II.

The pigeon pilot project illustrates Skinner's technological turn of mind. He was interested in practical applications of scientific knowledge. But at the same time he was interested in basic scientific understanding. Both of these objectives were furthered by discovering ways to condition more effectively the pecking behavior of pigeons. Most important in this was the discovery of the basic procedure which has become known as "shaping." One day Skinner and his associates taught a pigeon to bowl (with toy pins in a miniature alley) by carefully rewarding responses which ever more closely approximated the desired form of behavior. In analyzing their rather spectacular success, Skinner recognized the importance of using a reinforcer that could follow a response instantly. For this particular occasion they were using a mechanical food dispenser whose noises provided a conditioned reinforcer for the pigeon's actions. The results showed the importance of immediacy of reinforcement for the acquisition of new behavior or "learning." But there was another key lesson in what they had done. By reinforcing crude approximations of the desired behavior they obtained successful responses much earlier than if they had waited for the response to first occur naturally. And thus shaping, a basic principle for the modification of behavior, was discovered.

During the 1940s and 1950s Skinner increasingly turned from rats and pigeons to human beings as subjects for his analysis of behavior. In the most famous of his early work with human behavior he used his own daughter as the subject. He married Yvonne Blue in 1936, the same year that he went to the University of Minnesota. Two daughters, Julie and Deborah, were born to this marriage by 1945 when the Skinners moved to Bloomington, Indiana, where he was to chair the psychology department at Indiana University. At that time Skinner wrote an article in the *Ladies' Home Journal* describing the mechanical baby-tender he had devised for their second child. The "air-crib," as he called it, was a large sound-proof and air-conditioned box into which the baby was placed. By controlling the air intake, the baby box could be germ-free and at a constantly comfortable temperature. This made blankets or clothing for the baby unnecessary. A sliding panel of safety glass allowed the baby to observe freely the world outside, and she could be removed by opening this window. This baby-tending device was of course criticized by many who heard of it. Responded Skinner:

It is not, of course, the favorable conditions to which people object, but the fact that in our compartment they are "artificial." All of them occur naturally in one favorable environment or another, where the same objection should apply but is never raised. It is quite in the spirit of the "world of the future" to make favorable conditions available everywhere through simple mechanical means (Skinner, 1972, p. 572).

At about the same time he devised a special environment for his baby daughter, Skinner also devised an environment for an entire society. This took the form of his only published novel, *Walden Two*. It was three years before this book was published (several publishers had turned it down as being unlikely to arouse the interests of readers) but it soon became widely read, ultimately selling over a million copies. In this book a professor named Burris visits a scientifically planned utopian society. The dialogue between Burris and Frazier, the leading architect of the planned society, represented the issues to be faced in a scientific reconstruction of society. It also represented, as Skinner later admitted, "a venture in self-therapy in which I was struggling to reconcile two aspects of my own behavior, represented by Burris and Frazier" (quoted in *Time,* September 20, 1971, p. 50). In the end the liberal academic Burris swallows his doubts, and prepares to join the behavioral technologists at Walden Two.

The same year that *Walden Two* was published (1948) B. F. Skinner made a rather different move than had his hero Burris. It was at this time that Skinner returned to Harvard, to continue his career as an academic psychologist. And it was as a professor at Harvard that Skinner became generally recognized as the leading spokesman for operant psychology, behavior-modification procedures, and contemporary behaviorism.

Skinner's Operant Psychology

In the perspective of B. F. Skinner and his followers, there is no fundamental difference between social psychology and other fields of psychology. All psychology deals with behavior, and all behavior is a product of the environment in which it occurs. This is true alike for humans and for other animals. We start therefore not so much with a distinctively social (or even human) framework, but with a general framework that is increasingly applied to human social learning. This framework is most commonly termed "operant psychology."

All behavior, in Skinner's view, is a function of stimulus events. But early in his career he made a distinction between two fundamentally different forms of behavior: "respondents" and "operants." Respondents are behaviors that are mediated by the autonomic nervous system, while operants are those mediated by the central nervous system. It is therefore operant behavior which primarily involves the organism as a whole in its relation to the environment, and it is in such behavior that Skinner has been mainly interested.

For respondent behavior, all respondents are seen as a function of antecedent stimulus events. In contrast, operants are viewed as a function of events which *follow* the behavior. When stimulus events have the effect of increasing the probability that a response will occur again, this is called "reinforcement," or, more precisely, "positive reinforcement." Any increase in the rate of reinforced behavior is called operant conditioning.

Skinner developed a standard procedure for operant conditioning. First of all, a response must be identified for analysis. It is easier to study if this is a simple act, such as pressing a bar, but more complex actions can also be used. Second, there must be some assessment of the base-line rate of that response. How frequently does it occur naturally, that is, without any manipulation of conditions? Third, a potential reinforcer is selected and applied. We say "potential reinforcer" because we cannot yet be sure that it will really be a reinforcer. A reinforcer is any stimulus which strengthens (that is, increases the rate of) the response in question. If the response does not increase, whatever is applied is not a reinforcer; another potential reinforcer must then be used. Fourth, the reinforcing stimulus is systematically applied according to some predetermined schedule of reinforcement (for example, according to a fixed ratio to the responses emitted) until an increase in the response has clearly occurred. Fifth, the reinforcer is then withdrawn to see if the rate of response eventually changes back toward the base-line rate. If so, "extinction" is said to occur (that is, a decrease in strength of a conditioned response when it is no longer reinforced), and final demonstration is thus provided that the reinforcer selected was indeed responsible for the change in behavior. Given these five steps, the ability to apply operant conditioning to a given type of behavior is confirmed, and reinforcement may then continue to be used to manipulate that behavior.

When a behavior is only rarely emitted naturally, the above procedures have to be modified. Instead of waiting for the chosen response to occur before applying reinforcement, the reinforcer is presented whenever any tendency toward that response is made. Gradually the criterion for presenting the reinforcer is shifted to be closer and closer to the targeted response, until at last the selected response occurs with a frequency to allow its direct reinforcement. This process of reinforcing successive approximations to some final response is called "shaping."

So far we have spoken only of positive reinforcement. This is the kind of reinforcement Skinner and his followers have themselves used most consistently and recommended to others. But for completeness we must also recognize the presence of negative reinforcement and punishment. Here terminology is not always consistent, but it is now common to distinguish between negative reinforcement (removing a stimulus, usually an aversive one, when this removal makes a specified response more likely to occur) and punishment (presentation of a stimulus that makes a specified response *less* likely).

When reinforcement is made contingent upon a response,

and the frequency of that response increases, we may say that "learning" has occurred. Sometimes something similar occurs even though the reinforcement was not actually made contingent upon the response. That is, from the perspective of an outside observer, the reinforcement did not depend on the response; instead they just happened to occur together. Skinner recognizes that such chance events do cause changes in behavior, but he hesitates to use the word "learning" to apply to them. Instead he calls such behavior "superstition." But whether we speak of learning or superstition (that is, with the response-reinforcement relation either contingent or accidental) something in the reinforcement situation serves as a stimulus associated with reinforcement. This is the discriminative stimulus—S^D, in Skinner's shorthand notation. By associating this discriminative stimulus with other stimuli, we can obtain "generalization" (i.e., the occurrence of a response in the presence of stimuli other than those used in original conditioning). A somewhat opposite tendency can be created by differential reinforcement of similar responses (e.g., reinforcing a left turn but not a right turn). This will create "discrimination," a differential response for the two situations.

We have briefly presented the main concepts and ideas used in operant analysis. This is also sometimes called "behavioral analysis" or "the experimental analysis of behavior" as though these concepts provided *the* way to study behavior. The application of these concepts to the systematic manipulation of behavior (going beyond simple prediction of behavior to prediction *and control*) has become known generally as "behavior modification."

Skinner recognizes the difference between science and technology, between gaining knowledge about the world and using that knowledge to change the world. But to him there is little point in giving a great deal of attention to the difference.

Knowledge about the world comes in terms of functional relations of independent and dependent variables, or, in layman's terms, between causes and effects. The key to this knowledge is successful prediction. But prediction and control always go together. In order to have successful prediction of behavior, you need to have control of the conditions of behavior. And if the findings of science are to be given any practical application still more control will be necessary to shape the conditions that will bring desired changes. The step from "behavioral analysis" to "behavior modification" is therefore a very small step, and it is characteristic of Skinner and his followers that they are usually concerned with both analysis and modification of behavior.

Skinner's Science of Human Behavior

Skinner's original work in basic science was with rats and pigeons. Nevertheless, he never saw any reason why the basic principles involved were not equally applicable to humans. When he returned to Harvard in 1948, he organized a course on human behavior, which eventually served as the basis of the book *Science and Human Behavior* (1953). This book is more of a reasoned speculation about the possibilities of the operant analysis of man and society than it is a record of scientific accomplishments. Also there was then little to report on systematic behavior modification of humans. Since then the picture has changed considerably. The behavior modifiers are now at work in all kinds of settings—in prisons, mental hospitals, counseling settings, and schools. And everywhere there is talk about "positive reinforcement" and "contingency management."

Among the specific areas where operant psychology has been applied, it is in education that Skinner himself has been most active. He is generally regarded as the father of the "teaching machine" and programmed instruction. Actually, teaching machines of one sort or another have been around for many decades, but it remained for Skinner and his followers to develop them more systematically in the 1950s and 1960s. What Skinner did was to supply a detailed rationale for such behavioral engineering.

According to Skinner, a visit to his daughter's fourth-grade arithmetic class in 1954 was the direct inspiration for his teaching machine. What he had seen in that classroom was "minds being destroyed" (*Time,* September 20, 1971, p. 51), and he proceeded to develop mechanical devices that could be used to shape human learning more efficiently. The main factors in the success of his teaching machines, according to Skinner, were that:

(1) the student is frequently and immediately reinforced,

(2) he or she is free to move at his or her natural rate, and

(3) he or she follows a coherent sequence (Skinner, 1972, p. 182).

Since teaching is basically, in his view, "arranging contingencies which bring about changes in behavior" (quoted in Evans, 1968, p. 59), this can be more systematically arranged by machine than by a teacher in the normal classroom setting.

In moving from other animals to humans, a special interest of Skinner's was directed at the human use of language. He began to work seriously on a book on this subject in 1941, but it was not until 1957 that *Verbal Behavior* appeared in its final form. Immediately there was a storm of protest among scholars in linguistics and the humanities, for Skinner's analysis had apparently reduced complex linguistic behavior to operant conditioning. He himself admitted, only half in jest, that his book might have been subtitled *The Meaninglessness of Meaning* (Skinner, 1972, p. 347).

To demonstrate the plausibility of his key assumption that language behavior is acquired through a history of selective reinforcement, Skinner found it necessary in *Verbal Behavior* to make a distinction between two functions of language. One of these functions is direct need satisfaction, and the other is representation of the world. Direct need satisfaction creates what Skinner called "mands," verbal operants shaped by their consequences. These are the earliest forms of language behavior, and they continue dominant in emotive and imperative forms of language behavior. A slightly different process develops "tacts," which use language to represent the world. The approval of other persons is apparently the main source of reinforcement for the labeling and naming behaviors involved in tacts. Tacts are associated with particular discriminative stimuli, and their reinforcement is generalized rather than specific. This leads a person to behavior that uses language to label and describe his world rather than to obtain direct satisfaction. But even tacts, Skinner insisted, are developed through operant conditioning. We do not naturally name and describe things, but we acquire this behavior through a history of selective reinforcement.

Skinner has not drawn any line around what kind of behavior may properly be subjected to operant analysis, so long as it is behavior of an organism acting upon an environment. Hence there is nothing sacred about language behavior that would set it apart, so far as he is concerned. Another area which would be out of bounds for old-fashioned behaviorists, the self, Skinner has also felt should not be taboo. So long as some observable relationship between variables can be identified, Skinner is quite willing to welcome them into the field of behavioral science. Self-descriptive statements can be analyzed as operants in a manner similar to statements describing an external world. We may study, therefore, the way a person talks about himself and how these words may be functions of other events. It is not assumed, however, that there is any necessary structure to the self as a thing-in-itself. It is simply seen as a set of functional relations that involve self-descriptive behavior. The reinforcement that shapes self-descriptive behavior is primarily seen as the differential approval provided by other people.

Skinner's psychology, given its strong emphasis upon environmental determination of behavior, develops naturally into social psychology as he examines the conditions of human behavior. Social approval becomes a key "generalized reinforcer"—a class of stimuli allowing access to a variety of more particular reinforcements—that helps us understand most behavior which is distinctively social. But Skinner's psychology still remains the psychology of individual organisms. He may analyze human institutions, but they are still seen primarily in terms of the behavior of individuals. This approach may be illustrated by considering the one short passage in *Science and Human Behavior* where he deals with the subject of group dynamics. Here Skinner first of all dismisses the "group mind" idea with the assertion that "it is always the individual who behaves" (Skinner, 1953, p. 311). But how do we explain how members of a group come together in their behavior? Here he points to two key principles. The first is imitation. "Behaving as others behave is likely to be reinforcing"; we therefore generally learn to behave like others, other things being equal. The second key principle is the intensification of effects that come to an individual in a group. Each individual in a group finds his behavior more powerfully reinforced because his actions are made in concert with others. "The man attired in full uniform," for example, "parading smartly down the street, is re-inforced by the acclaim of the crowd even though it would not be forthcoming if he were marching alone" (p. 312). Through such mechanisms we can analyze group behavior as the product of the reinforcement histories of the individuals involved.

Skinner himself did little work in those specific areas most often identified as topics of social psychology such as childhood socialization, attitude change, interpersonal perception and attribution, or group dynamics. He would, in fact, consider many of the formulations in these areas as grossly unscientific by the standards of his science of behavior. In all of these fields, however, the work of Skinnerians—persons either directly or indirectly associated with Skinner's operant analysis of behavior—has been of growing importance.

Skinner's Philosophy of Behaviorism

Skinner presented new procedures and concepts for psychology. He has also clearly articulated a philosophy to go with his experimental analysis of behavior. In its broad outlines this philosophy is essentially the same that John B. Watson put forward a half-century ago to arouse Skinner's interest in psychology, and it still carries the name of behaviorism. But Skinner's statement of this philosophy is particularly eloquent, if extreme.

To begin with, Skinner's philosophy is scientific. And it is scientific in a radically empirical way. He wants to discover regular relationships between classes of observable events so that causal patterns can be established. In this he is not particularly interested in theory in the usual sense. In a famous article titled "Are Theories of Learning Necessary?" (Skinner,

1950), Skinner's answer to his own question seems to be "No." The phenomena of learning can best be studied in terms of simply analyzing functional relations of responses and previous conditions. This need involve no theory about what goes on between. Of course there is room for "theory" in the sense of summary statements of patterns of observed relationships, but there is no need for any appeal to mental processes to explain behavior. Behavior is always to be explained by identifying the objective stimulus conditions in which it occurs (including the past history of reinforcement of the organism).

Skinner may also be described as a proponent of "operationism," which he has defined as

. . . the practice of talking about (1) one's observations, (2) the manipulative and calculational procedures involved in making them, (3) the logical and mathematical steps which intervene between earlier and later statements, and (4) nothing else (Skinner, 1972, p. 370).

The major virtue Skinner sees in operationism for psychology lies in the fourth point: it helps us avoid excess baggage in getting on with the business of objective science. And whereas some varieties of operationism claim only public events (that is, events that may be externally observed and verified by others) as suitable for scientific analysis, Skinner sees no reason why some private events may not be included. The issue to him is not public vs. private but accessibility to observation. We can scientifically examine only what is accessible to observation, and perceptual responses and self-descriptive behavior provide examples of such supposedly private behavior that might be open to some forms of careful observation. But this does not need any addition of subjective categories for explanation. It is still by observable antecedent conditions that subsequent responses—public or private—must be explained.

It may be argued that Skinner does not always practice the science that he preaches. It is true that he does not limit himself exclusively to scientific work as characterized by his principles of operationism. However, his most specifically scientific work is a model of the operationism he preaches. And he recognizes his other writings as either showing plausible extensions of his scientific work (such as in *Verbal Behavior*) or as expressive of his scientific philosophy (such as *Beyond Freedom and Dignity*).

In such works as *Beyond Freedom and Dignity,* Skinner shows himself as not only an able scientist and exponent of a particular way of doing science; he also shows himself to be a lucid philosopher of human affairs. Not surprisingly, his main themes show a clear relationship to what he has discovered in the psychological laboratory. Let us attempt to summarize briefly the main content of this recent book.

To solve human problems we must effectively apply some kind of technology, Skinner maintains. But problems of human behavior cannot be solved through physical and biological technology; a technology of behavior is also needed. Many people, however, resist a technology of behavior. They resist it because they don't think it can be effective, and they resist it because they don't think it is desirable. Both of these objections can be seen to be grounded in the concept of "autonomous man"—the idea of a self-acting inner being that causes behavior. Because behavior is internally caused, this popular idea holds, a technology of behavior cannot be effective. Or, alternately, even if it could be effective, it wouldn't be desirable, for it would destroy the central values of the freedom and dignity of the individual.

But, counters Skinner, an experimental analysis of behavior gives us no reason to posit such an autonomous inner being. On the contrary, we see that behavior is controlled by environmental conditions. The concepts of freedom and dignity may themselves be better understood within a framework of environmental determinism than as expressions of some autonomous thing within. A "struggle for freedom" represents behavior characteristic of animals seeking to avoid or escape from aversive circumstances. A "sense of dignity" represents what is attributed to an individual, or what the individual attributes to himself or herself, because the conditions of behavior are not fully understood. A need for such freedom vanishes as aversive conditions are eliminated, and dignity becomes irrelevant as behavior becomes more fully explained. In any event, there is no reason to see either freedom or dignity as the result of some inner force. We must therefore overcome the way of thinking that sees desires for freedom or dignity as necessary bars against the development of effective behavioral technology.

A behavioral technology is not a dream. According to Skinner, it is already in the process of development. Its key is in the management of contingencies of reinforcement. But toward what ends do we wish to shape behavior? To provide more consistent positive reinforcement is Skinner's rather simple answer. The objectives of such consistent positive reinforcement can in turn be categorized as three types of values or "goods": (1) those things that have become goods because they aid biological survival, (2) those things that have become goods because they help others, and (3) those things that are goods because they assist a culture to survive.

The first two categories are not quite so controversial as the third. We can generally agree on the desirability of measures to assist health and safety and those that increase social responsibility (even though we may not agree how these may be best achieved, given the evidence at hand), but how are we to assist a culture to survive? Skinner has a formula to answer this question too: we must "accelerate the development of

practices which bring the remote consequences into play"
(Skinner, 1971, p. 143). For just as in the process of biological evolution those kinds of organisms that are more sensitive to the consequences of their action are most apt to survive; so too in the evolution of culture those forms will survive
that bring people under control of the fullest range of the consequences of their behavior. This may be used as the guiding
principle for the design, or redesign, of an entire culture.

In all of this, there is no need to balk at the concept of "control." Every time we systematically act upon the environment
in order to affect others we exert control. The main problem is
to be more clear about the *objectives* of control and to be more
effective in selecting the *means* of control.

And what becomes of our image of the nature of man—this
being who is now, according to Skinner, progressing beyond
the necessity of concern for freedom and dignity? Man is not
abolished. He continues to live as a species and as an individual. But his behavior is no longer seen as something that comes
from within. It is seen instead as a function of environmental
contingencies. "But does man not then become merely a vic-
tim or passive observer?" Skinner asks, and he proceeds to
answer:

He is indeed controlled by his environment, but we must remem-
ber that it is an environment largely of his own making. The evolution of a culture is a gigantic exercise in self-control. . . . We
have not yet seen what man can make of man (Skinner, 1971,
p. 215).

Skinnerian Social Psychology

As the prominence of B. F. Skinner, his operant psychology,
and behavior modification have all grown in the last half of the

twentieth century, they have increasingly become controversial. Skinner has often been bitterly attacked, with his behaviorism seen as the antithesis of distinctively human behavior ("rat psychology!") and his emphasis upon behavioral technology considered incompatible with humane or democratic values ("fascistic!"). In response to the attacks, Skinner has become even more of a public figure, appearing frequently in lectures or on television to join in the public dialogue. In his later years his efforts have mainly been in the direction of explaining his scientific philosophy. His recent books, *Beyond Freedom and Dignity* and *About Behaviorism,* are examples of this direction of his attention. He has increasingly left laboratory work to others, believing that his main contributions there have already been made. Likewise for central topics of social psychology: Skinner has given a general framework for the analysis of social behavior, but he has left it for others to fill out the details.

Among the areas of social psychology where Skinner's influence has recently been active has been that of beliefs and attitudes. At first glance this would seem an unlikely place to find a behavioristic approach. Attitudes are usually seen within the framework of a cognitive psychology, which eludes reduction to behaviorism. But how are attitudes learned? Is it not essentially through social reinforcement? And, a behaviorist might maintain, cannot their continuance and change best be seen in terms of the principles of operant psychology?

Perhaps the most significant recent work in the area of attitudes that bears a strong Skinnerian stamp is the self-perception theory of Daryl Bem. Starting with Skinnerian assumptions about the way we learn to label events in the environment, Bem goes on to suggest that the same processes also apply to the way a person identifies his or her own beliefs and attitudes. Through the differential reinforcement by other people the child develops habits of identifying objects in the environment according to the conventions of his or her language community. Similar processes of learning can also be applied to inner events. We learn to identify hunger, thirst, or "butterflies in our stomach" from the linguistic cues others have suggested to us and that they apply to the different conditions in which they have observed us. And we come to use these labels, first derived from others, as the framework for perceiving ourselves.

So far Bem's theory of self-perception is essentially the same as G. H. Mead's theory of the emergence of self. But Bem goes on to carry the theory toward a more radical behaviorism than Mead would have allowed. Mead assumed a relatively stable structure of the self based upon internalized expectations from a "generalized other." Bem sees less need to posit any stable internal structures; instead the individual can be seen as constantly reevaluating himself on the basis of the perceived effects of his own behavior. From our own behavioral cues, including the conditions under which our behavior occurs, we infer the internal states that we label as attitudes or beliefs.

An especially important distinction Bem makes concerns our identification of conditions under which behavior (including the expression of attitudes or beliefs) occurs. Does the behavior appear coerced or directly controlled by external conditions of reinforcement? If so, we learn to identify the behavior as externally determined and not as genuinely expressing actual beliefs or attitudes. On the other hand, when behavior is not so obviously externally controlled, we attach greater internal significance to it as an indicator of "real" attitudes and beliefs. Thus by learning to differentiate between different degrees to which behavior is associated with external constraints, we come to differentiate different degrees to which we see attitudes and beliefs (of other people and of ourself) as genuinely expressed.

From such considerations, Bem derived the key postulates of his self-perception theory, namely:

(1) Individuals come to "know" their own attitudes, emotions, and other internal states partially by inferring them from observations of their own overt behavior and/or the circumstances in which this behavior occurs. . . .

(2) To the extent that internal cues are weak, ambiguous, or uninterpretable, the individual is functionally in the same position as an outside observer, an observer who must necessarily rely upon those same external cues to infer the individual's inner states (Bem, 1972, p. 5).

In applying these postulates, Bem directly challenges the assumptions of cognitively based attitude theories. Cognitive dissonance theory has been an especially favorite target, with Bem arguing that the experimental results dissonance theorists use to support their case can be more simply interpreted by his self-perception theory. We will not go into an analysis here of the experimental literature on this issue. Suffice it to say that scientific controversy is still keen between cognitive dissonance and self-perception interpretations. Among the advantages of the self-perception theory is its simplicity; it requires no internal cognitive state to explain observed effects. It thus represents a more behavioristic approach to understanding attitudes than other social psychological theories. Whether or not it better accounts for the experimental data is a question we will not try to answer here.

Bem's work illustrates the extension of Skinnerian psychology into areas of social psychology generally regarded as domains for cognitive theorists. Others have used Skinner's work as a basis for invading more sociological areas of social psychology. The work of sociologist George C. Homans is especially prominent here.

The main contribution of Homans has been his attempt to build a bridge between the principles of operant psychology and the study of groups and organizations. "Elementary social behavior" is the name he has used for this area as he has attempted to build a theory of the elementary processes of human society (Homans, 1961, 1974). For others this area is usually identified as "exchange theory," following from Homans' basic image of social behavior as exchange (Homans, 1958).

The nature of Homans' exchange theory can best be seen by examination of his central propositions (Homans, 1974, pp. 16–39), which he states as follows:

(1) For all actions taken by persons, the more often a particular action of a person is rewarded, the more likely the person is to perform that action. . . .

(2) If in the past the occurrence of a particular stimulus, or set of stimuli, has been the occasion on which a person's action has been rewarded, then the more similar the present stimuli are to the past ones, the more likely the person is to perform the action, or some similar action, now. . . .

(3) The more valuable to a person is the result of his action, the more likely he is to perform the action. . . .

(4) The more often in the recent past a person has received a particular reward, the less valuable any further unit of that reward becomes for him. . . .

(5) When a person's action does not receive the reward he expected, or receives punishment he did not expect, he will be angry; he becomes more likely to perform aggressive behavior, and the results of such behavior become more valuable to him. . . . When a person's action receives reward he expected, especially a

greater reward than he expected, or does not receive punishment he expected, he will be pleased; he becomes more likely to perform approving behavior, and the results of such behavior become more valuable to him.

The language of these propositions is not exactly what Skinner would prefer. Homans' style is not as strictly behavioristic as Skinner's, and he feels free to talk about such things as what a person "expects." Still, the basic assumptions here are, as Homans claims, essentially those suggested by operant psychology. What Homans does is to build from these propositions to explain such group phenomena as conformity processes, communication patterns, status systems, and conflicts concerning notions of equity.

Our citation of the work of Bem and Homans is not meant to indicate that either would define himself primarily as a disciple of B. F. Skinner, though Homans (1961, p. 140) has identified Skinner as his favorite psychologist. Rather we have used them as examples of leading social psychologists who take a good deal of inspiration from Skinner and who explicitly acknowledge this debt. In no way, however, does either feel he must be limited to the language of Skinner's operant psychology.

Meanwhile, there is also a growing influence in social psychology of those who follow more simply and directly in a Skinnerian tradition. Examples of this may be seen in the increasing concern for human social behavior within the operant tradition (see, for example, Ulrich and Mountjoy, 1972, or Staats, 1975) as well as the extension of behavior modification to new kinds of behavior (see, for example, Hamblin, 1971).

Meanwhile, B. F. Skinner continues to elucidate his operant psychology and philosophy of behaviorism. He recognizes his behaviorism as a working hypothesis, but he has "no doubt of the eventual triumph of the position—not that it will eventually be proved right, but that it will provide the most direct route to a successful science of man" (Skinner, 1967, p. 410). Although a full confirmation of this basic faith of Skinner's is not at hand, operant behaviorism has made a sufficient impact in social psychology that it is at least one of the most important approaches toward building a science of human social behavior.

VI

THE BLINDNESS
OF THE MASTERS

Being a master of anything tends to carry with it a certain single-mindedness of purpose. There is a resolve to forge ahead in whatever is the chosen line of activity. Those we have recognized as masters of social psychology have forged ahead in laying frameworks for the analysis of social behavior. This has required originality and audacity, and with the audacity has come, for each, a certain blindness. For a way of seeing is also a way of not seeing, and all of our masters—Sigmund Freud, George H. Mead, Kurt Lewin and B. F. Skinner—have in some respects been limited in their perspectives by the very genius of their breakthroughs.

Let us start with Skinner. His approach has often been labeled as one-sided, extreme in what is left out of consideration; and indeed there is good reason to consider it just that. At a number of critical junctures Skinner rather arbitrarily appears to take one particular choice for his approach. At any rate, from the standpoint of logic and the interests of complete understanding, these choices appear arbitrary; but there is also a clear thread running through these choices. At each juncture Skinner chooses to deal with what is most easily observable and manipulatable. The result is a rather practical emphasis and a certain consistency in operant social psychology—but at the expense of a wide range of neglected subject matter.

To indicate some of the points at which Skinner turns a blind eye to phenomena others would consider important, let us start with his behaviorism. Skinner chooses to focus upon the whole-body behavior of organisms. Why not limited physiological responses, such as neurological patterns? Why not patterns of perceptual organization? Why not some supra-individual unit for analysis of behavior in a social system? Skinner cannot exclude any of these areas of scientific concern on completely logical grounds. What he must say instead is that he personally isn't very interested in these kinds of questions and/or that he doesn't think that they are as scientifically productive as his behavioral approach. And why aren't they as productive? Because they aren't as likely to help us understand behavior! It may be sensible to make behavior the focus of our analysis, but it is not logically self-evident.

A second limitation of Skinner's is his empirical preoccupation with the rate of behavior. This he justifies in that a rate is the best empirical indicator of the probability of a given kind of act. But two things should be recognized here. First, the idea of probability applies to general classes of behaviors, not to unique behavioral events. We are thus setting aside the quest for the full understanding of any particular behavior. Second, the frequency or rate of a given act is never quite the same as its probability. Logically, at least, there is a gap between most notions of probability and response rate. To give a somewhat extreme example: suicide is so probable that it is certain for a man who has placed a loaded revolver against his temple and pulled the trigger, yet for him there is no rate for such behavior. Or, on the other hand, for a man who has just given up a job on the assembly line, his recent rate of certain on-the-job actions bears no predictive power for his future responses. Now it may be that generally the rate of a response is the best indicator available for predicting the probability of that behavior, but it isn't *always* so. Likewise, the probability of a behavior may be the most important thing to know about behavior for purposes of practical prediction and control; but for certain kinds of understanding a probabilistic approach to knowledge may be short-sighted. For example, the details of a pitcher's style are not fully contained in his earned-run average; nor is his team's triumph in victory or disappointment in defeat adequately summed up by a won-loss record. Behavioral science, no less than baseball, sometimes requires us to attend to the full concrete detail of selected events.

A third point of arbitrary exclusion by Skinner of areas for investigation is his systematic environmentalism. For him behavior is always a function of environmental conditions. Behavior always occurs in an environment, and behavior changes as the contingencies provided by the environment change. But could there not also be internal contingencies affecting behavior? Skinner leaves these out of consideration, preferring to deal with more manipulable external events. Then, after excluding consideration of such internal causes of behavior, he dogmatically attacks the idea that there may be some. Much of his *Beyond Freedom and Dignity* may be interpreted in this light.

Finally, Skinner's whole obejctive frame of reference may also be identified as one-sided. In particular, his exclusive concern with the object side of the subject-object dichotomy may be questioned. Consider, for example, the basic paradigm for operant conditioning. The scientist first examines the base-line rate of the behavior that is the object of study, and then proceeds to change contingencies of reinforcement. What the organism then does (that is, its rate of emitting the desired response) is systematically recorded. But the analytic attention here is all upon the responding organism. The full sequence of activity also involves the scientist, and why he or she desires to manipulate the behavior of another organism. But of course this is getting outside the objective frame of reference of operant psychology.

In key respects, then, Skinner's operant psychology systematically excludes or neglects considerations of potential importance. The focus upon the behavior of an individual organism acting as a whole neglects both physiological and sociological perspectives on behavior. His concern for rate of behavior neglects a detailed analysis of any particular behavioral event. His assumption that behavior is always under environmental control leads him to exclude examination of other possible causal factors. And his concern for scientific objectivity has led to focusing upon responses of experimental objects rather than upon the entire experimental process, including the experimenter. All of these appear to be built-in biases of Skinner's operant psychology. In one sense they are blind spots. But in another they represent strengths. For these very biases have helped operant psychology do what it can best do. They have helped to provide clarity and rigor in developing an intellectual base for the manipulation of behavior. What has been excluded is precisely what is not apt to be useful for understanding behavior change. To focus upon behavior itself is the first step in this direction. To focus upon a rate helps to conceptualize clearly what might be changed. To look for environmental causes leads to useful handles for manipulation. And this is further aided by emphasizing the object side of the subject-object continuum.

We have not exhausted the points where B. F. Skinner's social psychology represents a systematic one-sidedness. When we move beyond the basic elements of operant psychology to the world view contained in books of a more general nature such as *Walden Two* and *Beyond Freedom and Dignity* there are numerous other criticisms that could be leveled. Among such criticisms is his naivity about establishing institutional structures in society, which is hardly answered by general comments about constructing a culture. Or we could criticize the philosophical basis of his assumption of determinism. But enough has been said by others on Skinner's limitations as a sociologist or philosopher. Our main point is that these limitations are closely interwoven with his strengths. Behind all the accusations of one-sidedness, we see a strong individualist with a technological cast of mind who resolutely turns his genius in the direction of a psychology of prediction and control of behavior. As applied to social psychology, the result has been a most practical social psychology—practical at least in the sense of providing effective tools for changing human behavior.

Freud's position in many ways is the direct opposite to that of Skinner's. Where Skinner deals with environmental forces, Freud probes for influences deep within the psyche. Where Skinner deals with external behavior, Freud concerns himself primarily with the organization and expression of emotional reactions. Where Skinner emphasizes the careful operationalization of measured variables, Freud used highly intuitive devices for labeling and explaining human psychodynamics. But there are also characteristics Skinner and Freud have in common. Both share essentially deterministic assumptions about human behavior that give rise to one-sided applications of their theories. And both base their theories clearly upon the individual, leading to only indirect consideration of social institutions and cultural systems.

For Skinner, behavior is thoroughly determined by the environment. For Freud, determinism is seen as primarily from within the psychological apparatus. But both show a faith that all behavior can be completely explained if we identify the true causal forces. They have both considered such faith as a primary assumption of science. Still, we should point out that such a deterministic faith is not a necessary assumption for science. We can go about building explanatory models without assuming that they should apply perfectly; we can identify causes of certain events without assuming that they totally determine such events; we can even assume that all events have a certain emergent quality that is never completely determined by the forces of preceding events. This is not to say that a philosophical indeterminism is preferable to determinism as an operating assumption for the working scientist. It is only to say that the theoretical and empirical activities of science do not require such a deterministic assumption. And it is also to imply that where such an assumption is freely made, there is a real danger that it may be applied in a one-sided manner. Freud's psychic determinism may be seen as a good example of this.

For Freud everything seemed to express inner psychological needs. Innocent slips of the tongue or of the pen were never quite so innocent, for they expressed important unconscious needs, he believed. And dreams too displayed the forces of this psychic determinism. There were no meaningless dreams—each one was organized by some central unconscious wish. Even complex phenomena of group action was for Freud based on the needs of these psychic structures, especially according to the way they were preconditioned by early relationships with parents. This concern for explaining behavior in terms of internal determinants led Freud to his theory of instincts, providing conceptual entities which could be freely used to express a causal closure for any occasion.

Skinner and Freud are also similar in that both have used essentially individualistic assumptions as the foundation of their approaches. For Skinner it is always the individual organism that behaves in response to environmental contingencies. For Freud it is also the individual who is always the unit of analysis. When this individual framework is combined with Freud's psychic determinism, the result is a highly egoistic view of human behavior. Behavior is generated by internal impulses seeking satisfaction, with drives of sex and aggression (both viewed in primarily self-seeking terms) central for the understanding of man's behavior with his fellow men. When Freud found difficulty in harnessing all social behavior to these primary drives, his response was to conceptualize another drive which would serve as their counterpoint—the death instinct. But here too the impulse was presented as based on internal strivings of the individual.

In his specifically social psychology, Freud relentlessly reduces complex social forms to expressions of libido. Thus religion and moral codes, in *Totem and Taboo,* derive from early forms of the Oedipal complex, as do the patterns of group interaction conceived in *Group Psychology and the Analysis of the Ego.* It is not surprising that such an approach would yield a one-sided social psychology. But what is surprising is that psychoanalytic insights have proved such a rich source of hypotheses for social psychology as they have.

We have found Freud similar to Skinner in his deterministic assumptions and his individualism. In most matters of content, however, we find Freud and Skinner almost polar opposites, with Freud focusing upon internal processes and Skinner upon external behavior. This difference in content is closely related to a contrast in method. While Skinner espouses, and fairly consistently has practiced, a scientific method closely akin to that of the natural sciences, Freud's science has a much more subjective character. Freud's method was empirical in a broad sense. He systematically probed to get new evidence on the operation of psychic forces. But there was never a systematic empirical test of his hypotheses. There were no systematic comparisons between experimental treatments and controls. There was no search for the possibility of disconfirming evidence, which is sometimes seen as the touchstone of scientific method. Instead we have a close-knit circle of psychoanalysts devoted to using Freud's ideas and methods—and to preserving them from the error of alternative interpretations.

In one sense Freud was a master scientist, probing fearlessly where others were too timid to explore. He was also imbued with the scientific assumption that man should use his reason to the maximum in pushing back the boundaries of the unknown. This was his primary mission in developing psychoanalysis. Freud was deeply imaginative in the manner in which he explored psychological foundations of behavior, seeking to explain what others would have considered inconsequential. But there was another side of Freud that was resentful of any challenge. Once a theory had been formulated, it became a kind of orthodox position for Freud's band of followers. And no one was to question the theory unless the master himself were to revise it.*

George H. Mead and Kurt Lewin are less obvious candidates for pointing out systematic blind spots than are Skinner

---

* Fromm (1949, pp. 62–67) presents some vivid illustrations of this authoritarian tendency of Freud's. Most telling is the incident where his disciple Ferenczi described to him some new approaches he was using in psychotherapy. Not only did Freud express his disapproval of Ferenczi's innovations, but he also refused to shake hands in departing. Another example of this authoritarian tendency may be found in The Freud/Jung Letters (McGuire, 1974) showing Freud's attitude toward Jung's innovative theories.

and Freud. Mead and Lewin seem more moderate, less extreme. Perhaps this is because their approaches are closer to the mainstream of contemporary social psychology. Their positions are generally quite compatible with each other, and each represents a dominant part of the history of modern social psychology. Mead is the most cited central figure in the tradition of sociologically trained social psychologists; and Lewin occupies a somewhat similar place among those trained more in psychology. Perhaps the central biases and preoccupations of Mead and Lewin are therefore less noticeable because they tend to be shared more widely. Even if this is so, we should be able to suggest what are some of these preoccupations and how they may continue to bias the attentions of social psychologists.

From a social science point of view, perhaps the strongest objection to Mead is that he was not a social scientist. He was by profession a philosopher, and his expression of basic ideas often took the form of a belabored philosophical discourse. The empirical referents, at any rate, were usually not made very clear. Translating Mead's ideas into the research of social psychology has frequently been difficult to achieve because of the general nature of his analysis.

But the problem of relating Mead to research goes deeper than his philosophical style. As we stated in Chapter Three, the central social psychological ideas of Mead are probably by nature untestable. For example, the assumption that the self arises out of social interaction is certainly a key idea, and we can find evidence that self-conceptions undergo change with changes in social interaction. But to say simply that the self arises through social interaction—period—is to shut out rather arbitrarily a search for other factors that might be involved. And to say that language is *the* basis of an internal organization of action is also perhaps to oversimplify. Jean Piaget, for

example, while in many ways similar to Mead in his treatment
of social factors, believes that nonsocial factors (such as experience with the physical environment and biological matura-
tion) are also important in the emergence of selfhood; and for
Piaget language is not the entire basis of self-reflective thought
(Piaget, 1970). The point here is twofold. On the one hand,
Mead made some central assumptions that may well have over-
stated the role of social interaction and language. But, on the
other, we cannot really prove or disapprove these assumptions.
We cannot do experiments of the scope necessary to test
whether or not self-conscious reflection would develop in a
sample of biologically normal humans (a) with extremely limited social interaction but a rich physical environment or
(b) with a rich variety of social interaction but without language as such. Without the evidence of such experiments, the
central ideas of Mead remain dogmas rather than scientific
generalizations. They may be convenient dogmas for social
psychologists to affirm—emphasizing the importance of distinctive social psychological perspectives—but they may also
lead to the neglect of alternative possibilities.

Another central feature of Mead's philosophic approach
was what might be considered a "constructionistic" bias. We
are referring here to the opposite of a reductionism, which
seeks to reduce complex behavior to elementary units. This
reductionism Mead systematically opposed. Man was not just
another animal; man was different from other animals in his
conscious organization of experience. Consciousness refers to
a quality of activity of the human organism that cannot simply
be identified with physiological or behavioral units. Such positions were central in Mead's point of view. They represent the
basis for his key contribution: a social theory of mind. But
they also point to limitations. Too sharp a distinction between
human behavior and that of other animals may lead us to neg-

lect the extent to which other animals might share key qualities of human experience—as has recently been demonstrated in teaching chimpanzees to use symbolic forms of communication. Too strong an emphasis upon constructed aspects of conscious experience may neglect the extent to which behavior responds rather directly to immediate stimuli. Too strong an emphasis upon the "generalized other" in the organization of norms may overstate both the consistency and the degree of internalization of these norms—resulting in what has been criticized as an "oversocialized" view of man.

One might speculate that the possible biases of George H. Mead we have mentioned have something to do with his early enthusiasm for the philosophy of Hegel. Here was a philosophy of process, of emergents, of wholes coming into being. This was a philosophy he saw as liberating himself from the limited individualist assumptions of his Protestant upbringing. Although he grew to abandon much of the particular content of Hegel's philosophy, there is something of Hegel's style of thought remaining in Mead's symbolic interaction. The self and the other constitute a kind of dialectic out of which a new self-consciousness may be born. And out of this process grow ever more comprehensive possibilities of what might come into being. John Dewey once remarked about Mead's "extraordinary faith in possibilities" (Dewey, 1931, p. 312)—of what might be brought into being through conscious action. That Mead, like Dewey himself, founded these upon the primary base of group action may well represent the continuing influence for both of them of a philosophical resolve to look at man constructively. Both saw humanity striving to bring to being ever more coordinated possibilities for social organization, which very much shared in the basic spirit of G.W.F. Hegel.

Lewin, like Skinner but unlike Freud and Mead, had a strong background in experimental psychology. Lewin had a genius for suggesting how experiments might be carried out with complex social phenomena. Also, like Skinner much of Lewin's experimentation was oriented toward producing change in behavior, what Lewin called "action research." In view of this, it is a bit surprising that Lewin's field theory lacks essential ingredients necessary for a predictive framework.

As we have pointed out in Chapter Four, field theory is unwieldy for use in a predictive manner. For one thing, its concern for the total field gives little basis for measuring what particular aspects might be most important within the field. Resisting statistical treatment of data, Lewin had a tendency to see truth in terms of general patterns—either a given case had a particular pattern or it did not. Thus the shades of gradation in measured variables, so important in most scientific prediction, tended to be neglected by Lewin. Finally, and perhaps most importantly, Lewin's field theory was ahistorical in character. It lacked clear identification of past events that could be indicative of future events.

Field theory is essentially a way of thinking about preparation for behavior. It is not a theory about what conditions lead to what effects. The particular content which is used for prediction is not given by field theory itself. It is added informally through a kind of clinical insight. That Lewin and his students were so successful in their experimental work stems at least as much from this clinical insight as from the more formal features of field theory, which is essentially empty of the content necessary to generate particular predictions of behavior.

One of the key limitations of field theory is that scientific prediction is difficult to obtain. Another is its phenomenological emphasis. The way a person perceives the world is essentially the framework used by Lewin for understanding his behavior. Neglected is anything a person would not be aware of. Lewin had little room for either the unconscious motives of Freud or the environmental contingencies of Skinner. The result was a one-sided emphasis upon conscious, cognitive factors at the expense of both the more deeply underlying and immediately overt aspects of behavior.

Still another systematic bias in Lewin's work was his consistent optimism about the group process. He did his best work through a group process, energetically involving himself with colleagues and students. And he tended to extend this same spirit upon his subject matter. Thus, group dynamics was not just a set of phenomena to be observed; group dynamics was also a way of changing the world. Groups were the framework of individual action, group decisions were more effective in changing behavior than individual decisions, democratic participation in decision making provided for more effective organizations, and so forth. There was a quality of ideological commitment here that went beyond neutral observation; but it cannot be doubted that this commitment added energy to his study of group processes.

In the present chapter we have been emphasizing the limitations of the perspectives in social psychology associated with our masters. We have noticed a rather gross one-sidedness in the perspectives of Freud and Skinner, but Mead and Lewin also have been seen as having biases in their perspectives. This, however, is not to downgrade the contributions of these masters. Indeed, the very limitations imposed by their biases have been intimately bound up with the special genius of each. Without his single-minded search for deeply rooted causes of behavior, Freud would not have given us his rich insight into the dynamics of the internalization of social forces. Without his basic commitment to a philosophical framework of emergence and construction—continually focusing on the way nature is built up by organized action—Mead would not have made his highly original analysis of the role of significant symbols. Without his basic commitment to looking at the total field of behavior and emphasizing the social content of that field, Lewin would not have done his pioneering work in group dynamics. And of course Skinner's single-minded attention to environmental factors in behavior change is responsible for the clarity with which his principles of operant psychology may be applied to social behavior.

So even while we criticize some of the limitations of Freud, Mead, Lewin, and Skinner, pointing to their blind spots or oversights, we must again recognize some of their special contributions. By narrowing their sights they were able to see more clearly certain features of social behavior, providing the distinctive insights that made them masters in this new science.

VII

PERSISTING PATTERNS
IN SOCIAL PSYCHOLOGY

Schools of thought are less clear in social psychology today than they have been in the past. There is more eclecticism, a greater borrowing from different traditions. But social psychology still shows the heritage of past masters in its predominant schools of thought. The main identifiable schools are behaviorism, cognitive theory, symbolic interactionism, and psychoanalysis. Behind each of these traditions are persons whose influence has been critical in the development of the school, with the names of Skinner, Lewin, Mead, and Freud standing out with special prominence.

Behaviorism as an approach in social psychology has always been associated with a desire for methodological purity. The basic rule is to deal with only what can be observed and measured. This leads to a focus on the behavior of organisms, and B. F. Skinner has most systematically made this behavioral focus the basis of his contributions. To study social behavior as shaped by its reinforcement contingencies is the obvious framework suggested for social psychology, and an increasing number of social psychologists are making this the main theme of their work.

But behaviorism is still not the dominant position in social psychology. Most feel that the preparation for behavior may be more important than overt acts in themselves. Among those social psychologists who have been trained in psychology departments, most give prominent attention to cognitive theories. How the individual subjectively creates the framework within which he or she acts is the key concern. And here the traditions of Gestalt psychology and Lewinian field theory are especially strong. It is not that many social psychologists use the terminology of Lewinian field theory any more (that has been largely abandoned) but the underlying assumptions that behavior is cognitively mediated, subjectively organized, and based especially upon an interpreted social environment—these are key themes following very much in the Lewinian tradition.

Research methodology is generally less simple in this tradition (there are quite often some slippery assumptions made in setting up variables to be measured), but the emphasis upon experimentation is still strong here. Science must be based on systematic empirical evidence observed under carefully controlled conditions, an assumption most cognitive social psychologists hold in common with behaviorists. The difference lies in what they are trying to build a science to *explain*. The behaviorists do not set their sights beyond accounting for patterns of frequency for forms of behavior. The cognitive theorists, on the other hand, seek to explain how the individual organizes his or her world subjectively in preparing to act.

Not all, but most sociologically trained social psychologists see themselves primarily within the framework of symbolic interactionism. Their response to behaviorism is similar to that of cognitive theorists with a psychological background. They too consider the preparation to act, including the internal organization of meanings, as more important than observing frequencies of different kinds of acts. Where symbolic interactionists mainly differ from most cognitive psychologists is in their emphasis on the social form and content of an individual's organization of meanings. These meanings are seen as directly rooted in patterns of symbolic usage, which in turn reflect the organized nature of society. In a sense, then, society is prior to the individual. Interaction is shaped by the organization of society, and the patterns that the individual takes on to shape his interpretations grow out of this social interaction. Not only is it important to note that the individual relates to a social environment in constructing a response, but the ingredients of construction—the very forms that cognitively shape social acts—are themselves distillations of past social interaction.

The profoundly social nature of the mind is the chief distinguishing theme of social interactionists—a theme that comes directly from George H. Mead. Methodologically, the symbolic interactionists are a diverse group, though most of them are less concerned about rigorous experimental design than are behaviorists or cognitive psychologists. Some, following the lead of Hubert Blumer, are skeptical of any analysis that deals with specific measured variables, insisting that it is the full interplay of concrete events that must be studied and not abstracted variables. Those insisting on this emphasis are more likely to use case studies, which are rich in describing the context of social interaction, than laboratory experimentation. Since there is a greater emphasis in this tradition upon the relativity of thought to the social context of the thinker, there is usually less weight given to specifically "objective" methods. Truth about behavior, it is held, is to be obtained more by grasping the full social context of an act than in reducing it to some feature that can be physically measured.

Then there is psychoanalysis. Very few academic social psychologists see themselves as primarily within the psychoanalytic tradition, but many find this tradition rich in useful ideas. Those who are strongly influenced by psychoanalysis may be found among sociologists and anthropologists as well as among psychologists. In fact, it is probably among anthropologists that the psychoanalytic approach has been most favorably received; at any rate, psychoanalytic conceptions of early experience in shaping personality have provided many hypotheses for anthropological investigation. Generally, however, social scientists have had difficulty with the biological and individualistic orientations of Freud's work, often leading them to prefer the looser formulations of the neo-Freudians. But both the Freudians and neo-Freudians are criticized on methodological grounds since the experimental tradition is quite foreign to either group. The clinical investigation and reasoned inference used by psychoanalysts is a far cry from the standards of evidence that are usually desired in psychology or in sociology. This factor as much as any accounts for the somewhat infrequent use of psychoanalysis by academic social psychologists. They view it as a useful basis for speculation, but resist giving its theories the status of scientific generalizations.

We have spoken of schools of thought in contemporary social psychology and characterized their relative influence. In so doing we have suggested something of the length of the shadows of the figures of our masters—Freud, Mead, Lewin and Skinner—upon social psychology today. This is not to suggest that any of these names would likely be mentioned in a typical article in a social psychology journal. Most studies focus upon much more specific questions than those we have given attention to in this book. But still, in most journal articles, there would be some degree of affinity with one of these general schools of thought in the way the problem is identified and attacked in that article.

To a degree the schools of thought we have identified may be considered as rival paradigms. Freud, Mead, Lewin, and Skinner have given us fundamentally different patterns for doing social psychology. But in another sense, these approaches need not necessarily be in conflict. The approaches of all four men are different in large part because they ask us to focus upon different aspects of reality. With this in mind, we may suggest that the complete social psychologist should be one who can combine these different approaches. Viewed in this fashion, they may be considered more as complementary approaches than as rivals.

Let us assume that all behavior always grows out of both (a) conditions of external relationships and (b) conditions of the internal functioning of individuals. Some of these conditions have a long-term influence upon the persisting patterning of behavior. Freud made us sensitive to internal psychological conditions that may affect persistent patterns of behavior, and Mead made us sensitive to the impact of external social relationships. Each emphasizes a different side of the coin, but for both the concern is primarily to identify *patterns in persistent behavior*—in personality or selfhood, not just in momentary responses of the person.

Somewhat different is the focus of Lewin and Skinner. Both of these have suggested a greater attention to the *immediate* conditions of behavior. Here too we have attention given to different sides of a process. Lewin focused upon the internal organization of events in his field theory, while Skinner's behavioral theory focuses on external relationships. The contrast between them is primarily that of a cognitive versus a behavioral emphasis in examining the conditions for ongoing behavior.

Classifying the approaches in this way, it becomes apparent how they may be complementary. Whether or not we follow the particular theories of Freud, Mead, Lewin, or Skinner, they all at least give attention to important aspects of behavior a full science of social behavior can hardly ignore.

In one sense, then, the masters of social psychology present us with competing ideas for the interpretation of social behavior. But in another sense we see the need in social psychology for something of all of these approaches. Each presents a way of handling questions largely omitted by the other approaches. For exploring the full range of questions about the social behavior of humans we neglect at great hazard the legacy of any of these masters.

REFERENCES

Backman, Carl W., Paul F. Secord, and Jerry R. Peirce. "Resistance to Change in the Self Concept as a Function of Perceived Consensus Among Significant Others," *Sociometry,* 26 (1963), pp. 102–11.

Bem, Daryl J. "Self Perception Theory." In L. Berkowitz, ed., *Advances in Experimental Social Psychology,* vol. 6. New York: Academic Press, 1972.

Costigan, Giovanni. *Sigmund Freud.* New York: Macmillan, 1965.

Dewey, John. "The Reflex Arc Concept in Psychology," *Psychological Review,* 3 (1896), pp. 357–70.

———. "George Herbert Mead," *The Journal of Philosophy,* 28 (1931), pp. 309–14.

Evans, Richard I. *B. F. Skinner: The Man and His Ideas.* New York: Dutton, 1968.

Freud, Sigmund. *The Interpretation of Dreams* (first published 1900), in *The Complete Psychological Works of Sigmund Freud,* vol. 4. London: Hogarth Press, 1953.

———. *On the History of the Psycho-Analytic Movement* (first published 1914), in *The Complete Psychological Works of Sigmund Freud,* vol. 14.

————. *The Ego and the Id* (first published 1923), in *The Complete Psychological Works of Sigmund Freud,* vol. 19.

————. *Group Psychology and the Analysis of the Ego.* New York: Liveright, 1922.

————. *An Autobiographical Study* (first published 1925), in *The Complete Psychological Works of Sigmund Freud,* vol. 20.

————. *Civilization and Its Discontents* (first published 1930), in *The Complete Psychological Works of Sigmund Freud,* vol. 21.

————. *New Introductory Lectures on Psycho-Analysis* (first published 1933), in *The Complete Psychological Works of Sigmund Freud,* vol. 22.

Fromm, Erich. *Sigmund Freud's Mission.* New York: Harper & Row, 1959.

Hamblin, Robert L. *The Humanization Process.* New York: Wiley, 1971.

Heider, Fritz. *The Psychology of Interpersonal Relations.* New York: Wiley, 1958.

Heilbroner, Robert L. *The Worldly Philosophers.* New York: Simon & Schuster, 1961.

Homans, George C. "Social Behavior as Exchange," *American Journal of Sociology,* 63 (1958), pp. 597–606.

————. *Social Behavior: Its Elementary Forms.* New York: Harcourt Brace, 1961 (rev. ed., 1974).

Kuhn, Manford H. "Self-Attitudes by Age, Sex, and Professional Training," *Sociological Quarterly,* 1 (1960), pp. 39–55.

Kuhn, Thomas S. "The Structure of Scientific Revolutions"; vol. 2, no. 2, of the *International Encyclopedia of Unified Science.* Chicago: University of Chicago Press, 1962.

Lewin, Kurt. *A Dynamic Theory of Personality.* New York: McGraw-Hill, 1935.

————. *Principles of Topological Psychology.* New York: McGraw-Hill, 1936.

————. *Field Theory in Social Science.* New York: Harper & Bros., 1951.

McGuire, William. *The Freud/Jung Letters: The Correspondence between Sigmund Freud and C. G. Jung.* Trans. Ralph Manheim and R. F. C. Hull. Princeton: Princeton University Press, 1974.

Marrow, Alfred J. *The Practical Theorist: The Life and Work of Kurt Lewin.* New York: Basic Books, 1969.

Mead, George H. "Social Consciousness and the Consciousness of Meaning," *Psychological Bulletin,* 7 (1910), 397–405.

———. "A Behavioristic Account of the Significant Symbol," *Journal of Philosophy,* 19 (1922), 157–63.

——— "The Psychology of Punitive Justice," *American Journal of Sociology,* 3 (1918), 577–602.

———. *Mind, Self, and Society: From the Standpoint of a Social Behaviorist,* edited by Charles W. Morris. Chicago: University of Chicago Press, 1934.

———. *The Philosophy of the Act,* edited by Charles W. Morris. Chicago: University of Chicago Press, 1938.

Mey, Harold. *Field Theory: A Study of its Application in the Social Sciences.* New York: St. Martin's Press, 1972.

Miller, David L. *George Herbert Mead: Self, Language, and the World.* Austin: University of Texas Press, 1973.

Miyamoto, S. Frank, and Sanford Dornbusch. "A Test of the Symbolic Interactionist Hypothesis of Self-Conception," *American Journal of Sociology,* 61 (1956), pp. 399–403.

Morris, Charles. *The Pragmatic Movement in American Philosophy.* New York: George Braziller, 1970.

Piaget, Jean. "Piaget's Theory," in Paul H. Mussen, ed., *Carmichael's Manual of Child Psychology,* 3rd ed. vol. I, pp. 703–32. New York: Wiley, 1970.

Quarantelli, E. L., and Joseph Cooper. "Self-Conceptions and Others: A Further Test of Meadian Hypotheses," *Sociological Quarterly,* 7 (1966), pp. 281–97.

Robert, Marthe. *The Psychoanalytic Revolution.* New York: Harcourt, Brace & World, 1966.

Rosenberg, Milton J. "The Experimental Parable of Inauthenticity: Consequences of Counterattitudinal Performance," in John S. Anthrobus, ed., *Cognition and Affect,* pp. 179–201. Boston: Little, Brown, 1970.

Rucker, Darnell. *The Chicago Pragmatists.* Minneapolis: University of Minnesota Press, 1969.

Skinner, B. F. *The Behavior of Organisms.* New York: Appleton-Century, 1938.

————. "The Operational Analysis of Psychological Terms, *Psychological Review,* 52 (1945), pp. 270–77.

————. *Walden Two.* New York: Macmillan, 1948.

————. "Are Theories of Learning Necessary?" *Psychological Review,* 57 (1950), pp. 193–216.

————. *Science and Human Behavior.* New York: Macmillan, 1953.

————. *Verbal Behavior.* New York: Appleton-Century-Crofts, 1957.

————. "Pigeons in a Pellican," *American Psychologist,* 15 (1960), pp. 28–37.

————. "B. F. Skinner," in Edwin G. Boring and Gardiner Lindzey, eds., *A History of Psychology in Autobiography,* vol. 5. New York: Appleton-Century-Crofts, 1967.

————. *Beyond Freedom and Dignity.* New York: Knopf, 1971.

————. *Cumulative Record,* 3rd ed. New York: Appleton-Century-Crofts, 1972.

————. *About Behaviorism.* New York, Knopf, 1974.

————. *Particulars of My Life.* New York: Knopf, 1976.

Staats, Arthur W. *Social Behaviorism.* Homewood, Illinois: Dorsey, 1975.

Thompson, Clara. *Psychoanalysis: Evolution and Development.* New York: Hermitage House, 1950.

Time Magazine. "Skinner's Utopia: Panacea, or Path to Hell?" Sept. 20, 1971, pp. 47–53.

Ulrich, Roger E., and Paul T. Mountjoy. *The Experimental Analysis of Social Behavior.* New York: Appleton-Century-Crofts, 1972.

Watson, John B. *Psychology from the Standpoint of a Behaviorist.* Philadelphia: Lippincott, 1919.

————. "John Broadus Watson," in C. Murchison, ed., *A History of Psychology in Autobiography,* vol. 3. Worcester, Mass.: Clark University Press, 1936.

Webster, Murray, Jr., and Barbara Sobieszek. *Sources of Self-Evaluation.* New York: Wiley, 1974.

INDEX